Rough Style

Architecture, Interior, Design

Rough Style

Sibylle Kramer

Architecture, Interior, Design

BRAUN

CONTENTS

PREFACE

Roughness in architecture means an esthetics which creates a very special charm with its uniqueness. It often conveys a transitory, big city mood which triggers curiosity about the spirit that fills these special spaces with life. The antitheses of old and new or a new interpretation of rudimentary materials belong just as much to this intriguing species as a contrast between perfect design and supposedly imperfect building materials.

This volume presents more than 100 exceptional buildings which display the rigors of rough esthetics. That can be the material itself, the way of handling the existing construction or technology, or it can be the degree of detail and the dialogue with the location which make the architecture rough. The common denominator of the projects is a uniqueness which offers leeway for one's own discoveries and pursuing the exciting trail of history. The selected projects show different ways of dealing with materiality and structural elements which establishes new standards for value in another context. A dilapidated and partially destroyed building shell is transformed into an architectonic jewel with a unique character, as the Lisbon Design and Fashion Museum (MUDE) by Ricardo Carvalho + Joana Vilhena Arquitectos shows. New counters and display surfaces play off the raw building shell and reinvigorate the building. Or an empty listed building is awakened from a Rip Van Winkle slumber through the intelligently implemented symbiosis of old and new: the otherwise ungainly insulation panels in the existing building, in tandem with old construction, modern elements made of glass and steel as well as the new inset airspaces come up with a new esthetics and an utterly different atmosphere, as the office spaces of Alphabeta, designed by hda – Henrik Diemann Architekten from Hamburg illustrate. Maria Flöckner and Hermann Schnöll from Salzburg detach simple panel material from the accustomed context and with the aid of tailored detail work obtain a completely new and high-end appearance. For the kitchen design in the T House the architects used simple OSB panels, which are normally assigned more humble tasks, like temporary dust screens or invisible sub-assemblies. Other projects display copper pipes, which

are usually hidden away, and that now gleam with unaccustomed splendor in front of a gray formwork concrete wall or old facing masonry. Furthermore, old and new are often paired together, complementing each other perfectly, achieving stunning results. In the process, recycling material is cleverly arranged and reinterpreted, the new context resulting in innovative and different usages. By placing focus on elements that are usually hidden from sight and integrating them into the design concept, the architecture and design presented in this volume create a new and powerful esthetics. What was once considered incomplete and in need of repair is chic and hip today. So get ready for some pleasant surprises and strong, convincing concepts that are perfected by their rough imperfection.

STRÖMKAJEN FERRY TERMINALS

Real Swedish grit frames the magnificent view over the old city of Stockholm.

Architects | Marge Arkitekter
Location | Stockholm, Sweden
Completion | 2013
Size | 322 sqm

The terminal buildings for the archipelago boat traffic are at Strömkajen – one of Stockholm's most frequented areas. It is the departure point for sightseeing boats. The design places priority on maintaining free views and highlighting the monumental edifices on Blasiholmen. The terminal buildings have been accordingly scaled down in deference to the surrounding architecture. The design concept is based on the elementary form of cones, which are either open, framing a view over the water, or closed in order to present traffic information. The cones are combined in different ways to meet the demands of the different businesses, resulting in buildings without any specific fronts and backs. Every building is unique but together they create a cohesive expression for the boat traffic of Strömkajen.

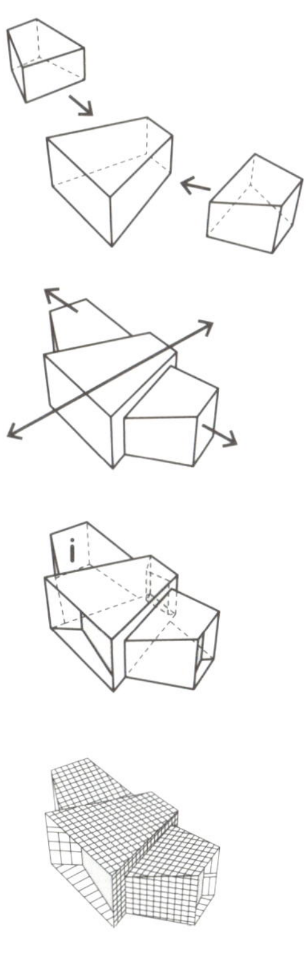

Exterior façades are covered with burnished Tombak, a brass alloy. The interiors are done in rough sawn oak. Glass sections in the waiting hall and the selling area are drawn back to provide shelter from the rain and space for facade display.

SVENSKA HANDELSBANKEN
STOCKHOLM SIGHTSEEING

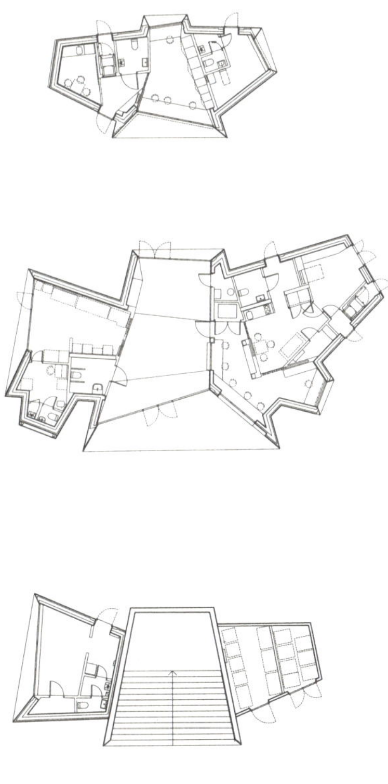

Architects | Sol89. María González & Juanjo López de la Cruz
Location | C/ Madre de Dios, Seville, Spain
Completion | 16th century / 2014
Size | 830 sqm
Original use | Convent of Madre de Dios de la Piedad

14

CONTEMPORARY ART SPACE IN AN OLD CONVENT

Art as the finishing piece of a building. Unconventional building methods put into practice.

The intervention interprets the building where it is inserted as a context in constant transformation over time. The project arises from a reflection around the creation process in contemporary art, its unpredictable condition and the current breakdown of limits between the space of production and exhibition. Much of contemporary art understands the architectural space as a matter of work, so the architects think that exhibition space shouldn't be projected like a static room in time but as a space which waits for each exhibition to complete it. The intervention will act as an initial installation in the space rather than an architectural construction. A temporary display relating to the existing volume that enables the development of future exhibitions and that can be disassembled.

Working with the layers of time existing in this place, the past is rediscovered through the scars of the brick walls, offering space for the contemporary art practice connected with the history of the old convent.

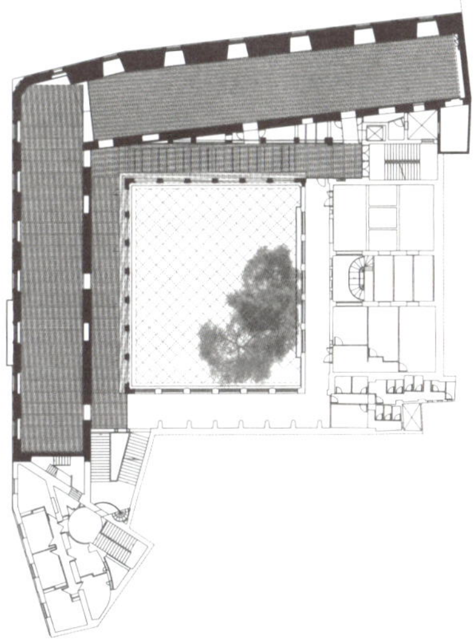

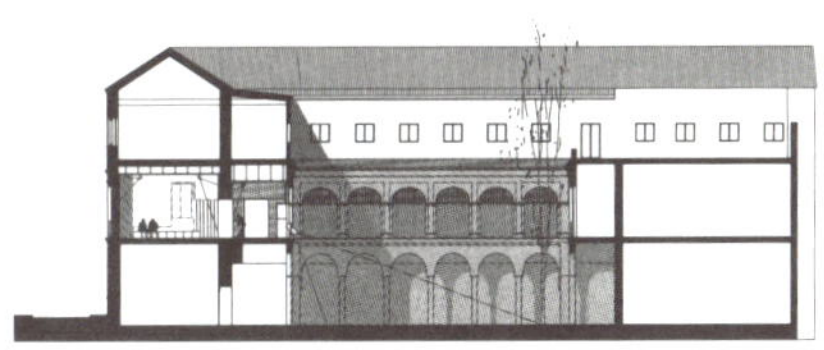

STEIN HOUSE

A smooth minimalist interior hidden behind a rough shell. Surprise, surprise!

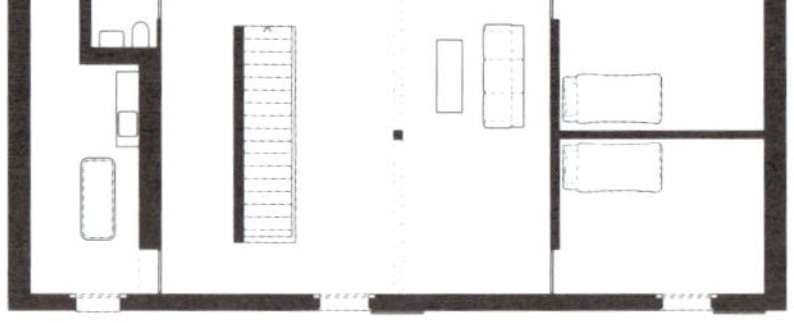

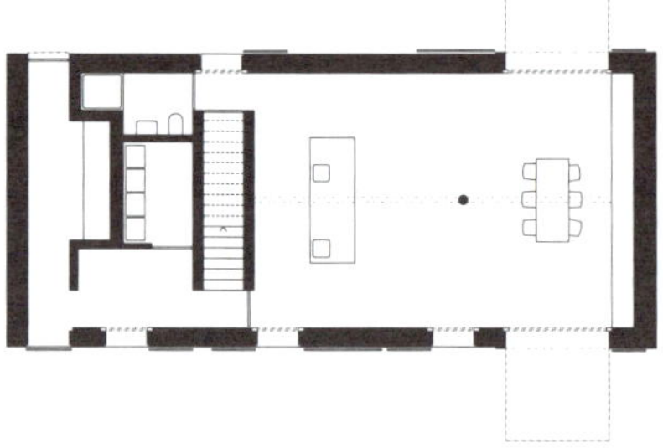

18

Architects | JAN RÖSLER ARCHITEKTEN
Location | Druxberge, Germany
Completion | 1930 / 2013
Size | 240 sqm
Original use | barn

Stein House is a brick barn from the 1930s that has been converted into a vacation house. The basic architectural concept was to maintain the appearance of the exterior. With slight interventions in the façade, the image of the building changes depending on the status of use. When the people are home, the warm light from the interior radiates from windows which are not perceptible from outside. When they are away and the wooden gates and shutters are closed, the house reverts to being a barn again. The vaulted ceiling over the ground floor dominates the interior design. The floor plan is divided in two areas. The ground floor is devoted primarily to daily routine with a kitchen/living room and dining area. The rooms upstairs are more intimate and use warmer materials.

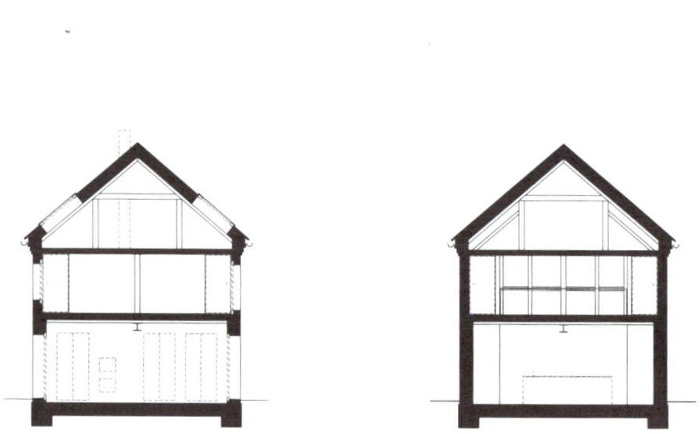

The architects prefer sustainable building materials like insulation made of wood or flax. The interior is plastered with permeable plaster and whitewashed in certain areas. Flooring made of wood and natural stone complete the chemical-free material concept.

Architects | March Studio
Location | Canberra, Australia
Completion | 2013
Size | 700 sqm

Located in NewActon, a diverse new precinct in Canberra, Nishi Commercial is a major new development housing government departments, private offices, a cinema and cafés. The lobby projects a unique identity through thousands of lengths of repurposed timber, blurring boundaries while directing views and movement. A grand stairway – the stage for performances as much as idle procrastination – leads up to the hotel lobby and bar. The timber in the stairs is a heavy stacked agglomeration. Freed to scatter up the walls and across the ceiling, the suspended timber filters exterior light and views into and from internal spaces. Spidery, pixellated shadows are cast on the floor and bare walls. The stair links Nishi Commercial to Nishi Residential, a multi-story apartment building housing two floors of hotel rooms wrapped around a central courtyard and light well.

22

HOTEL LOBBY AND NISHI GRAND STAIR INTERIOR

All for One, One for All. Creating a strong identity with 2,150 pieces of wood

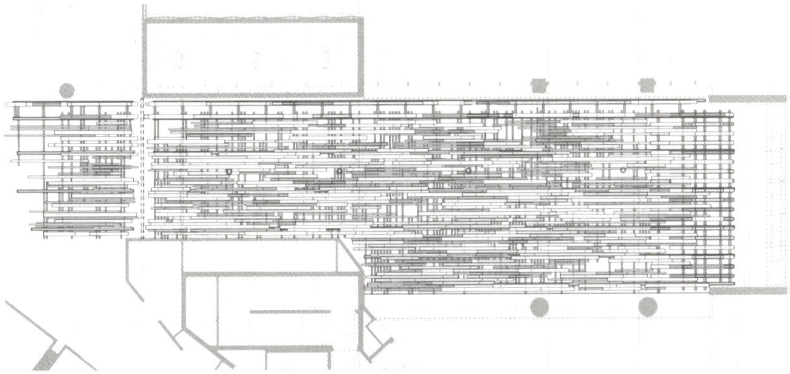

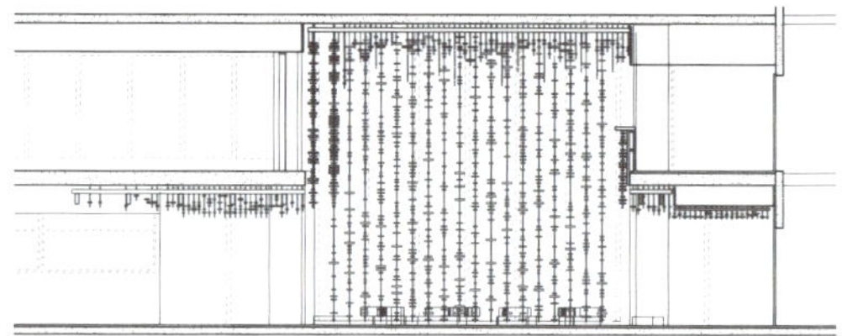

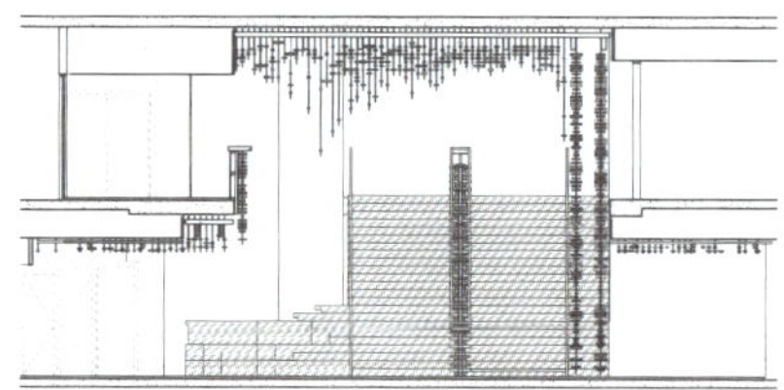

March studio's design process motto is "let the location inform the materials and let the materials inform the design." Hotel Lobby and Nishi Grand Stair Interior follows rigorously these rules. The creative inspiration was inspired directly by the construction site itself. All the reclaimed timber collected from the Nishi construction site itself were assembled to create the unique and majestuous sculptural interior.

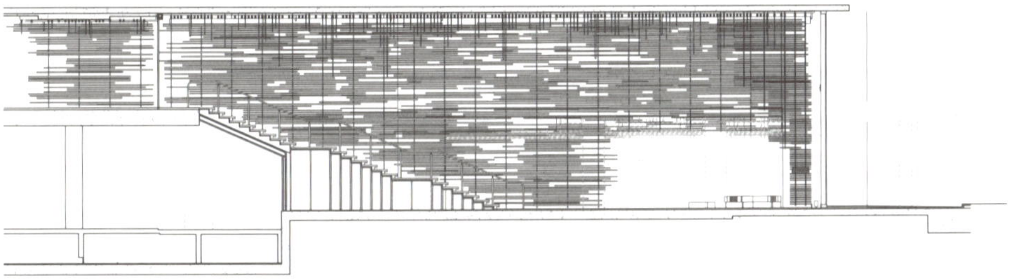

AUDITORIUM IN THE SANT FRANCESC CONVENT

Risen from the ruins. Who said a scar has to be a flaw?

Architects | David Closes architect
Location | Carrer del Convent, Santpedor, Catalonia, Spain
Completion | 1729 / 2011
Size | 950 sqm
Original use | convent

The Sant Francesc convent was built in the early 18th century. The project was aimed to convert the church of the convent into an auditorium and a cultural facility. The intervention has consolidated the church without disguising the process of deterioration and collapse that the building had suffered. The project maintained the interior dimensions of the church and the unusual incursions of natural light through the partially collapsed roof. Rather than reconstructing the church, the intervention has consolidated the old fabric, distinguishing clearly the new elements from the original ones. The renovation was carried out to read the historical wounds and maintain the building's most important spatial values without compromising the use of contemporary language in the new elements introduced in the intervention.

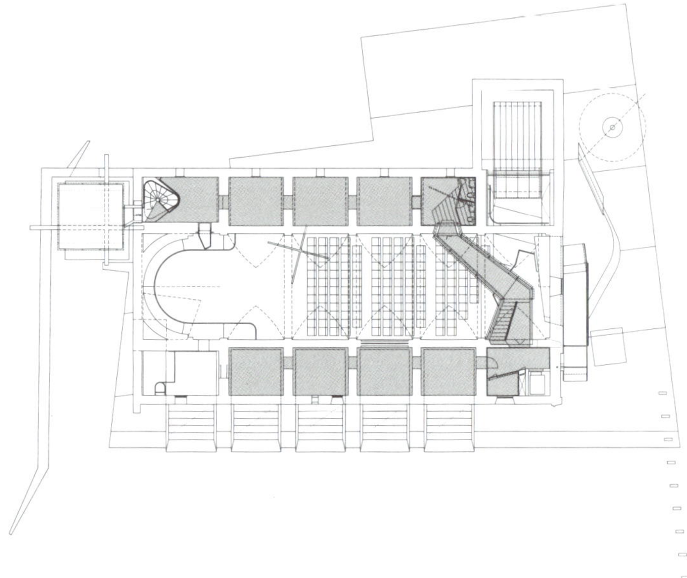

Each act of historic preservation carries a value judgment. Usually the architects choose which moment in history to preserve. Not here. In Sant Francesc there isn't a reconstruction of one historical moment; there is a preservation of history itself, as a complete and continuous fact. The maintenance of the wounds and scars of the building was an act of honesty regarding the entire history of the building.

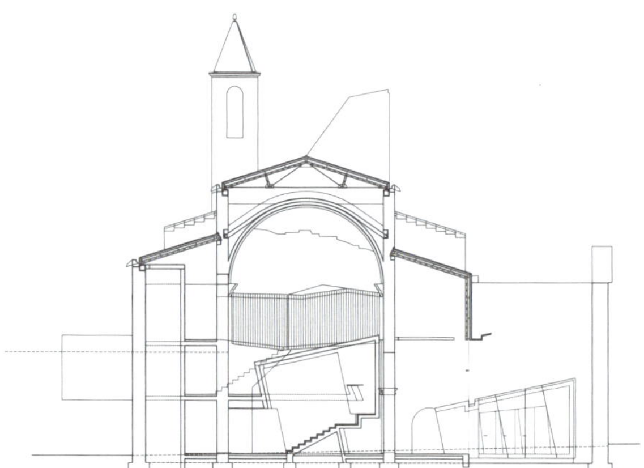

The historically listed NOCKI is a building to the rear of the slope of the Nockherberg in the Munich Au. Originally built in 1860 as a carpentry workshop, it was converted for residential purposes in the course of time with an annex and extra floor. After a fire in the 1990s it became an empty ruin. A figure made of insulating exposed concrete is woven into the ruin, replacing it where there was nothing left to preserve and plugging holes, surrounding the existing walls with a ring beam. The building has been extended by one room into the slope, opening up the formerly separate apartment units to light, air and the residents. The room contains all fittings, so that in addition to providing the static support, it is also the technical backbone of the building.

Architects | leonardhautum Lisa Hautum & Kristin Leonard
Location | Nockherstraße 27, 81541 Munich, Germany
Completion | ca. 1860 / 2012
Size | 100 sqm
Original use | carpentry workshop

NOCKI ... A PATCHWORK

Renovation, additions and continued building!
The tradition of the old Herbergshäusl goes on.

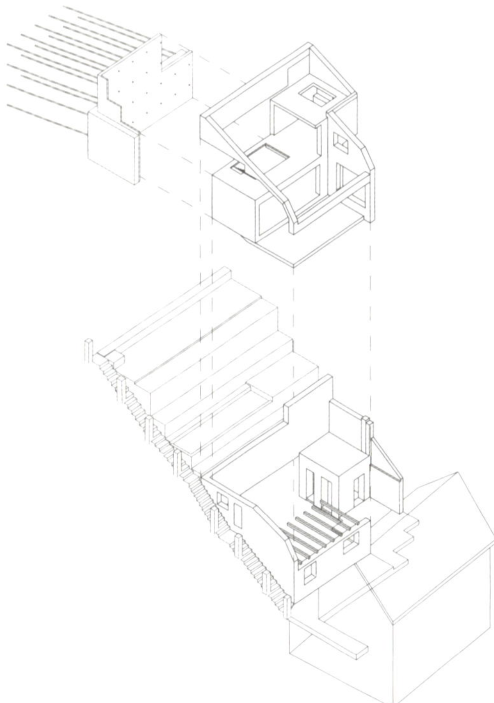

The heavily damaged condition of the ruins did not make discerning the Herbergshäusl's beauty easy. But there was no question about the more than 150 years old building segments – as much as possible had to be retained! In the architects' subjective staging, old and new elements have been fitted together in something entirely new, a historical PATCHWORK.

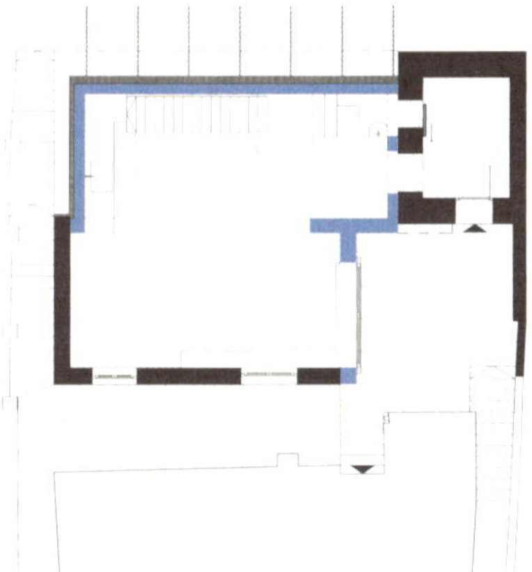

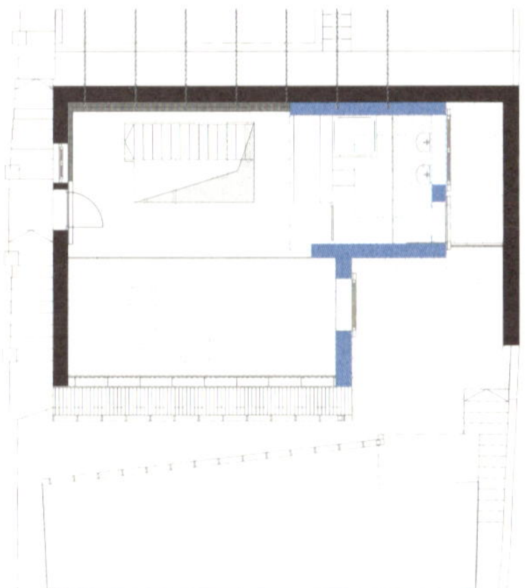

SUMMERHOUSE LAGNÖ

Three gables plus one gable equals two volumes or one summerhouse aka mini village.

Architects | Tham & Videgård
Location | Lagnö, Stockholm
Completion | 2012
Size | 140 sqm

The setting is the Stockholm archipelago, natural ground sloping gently down to the sea in the south, mostly open with a few trees and bushes. The architects searched for a way to design the house as an integral part of nature, where the material's weight and color scale connect to the bedrock granite of the archipelago. When approached from the north, the entrance presents itself as an opening between the buildings pointing towards the light and water. The exterior character of the house is derived from a number of transverse interconnected gable roofs, which like boathouses in a line form a long pleated façade. This construction provides a sequence of varied room heights for the interior and creates differentiations in the otherwise completely open living room that stretches through the entire length of the main building. The small rooms are located along the north façade with access through a wall of sliding doors.

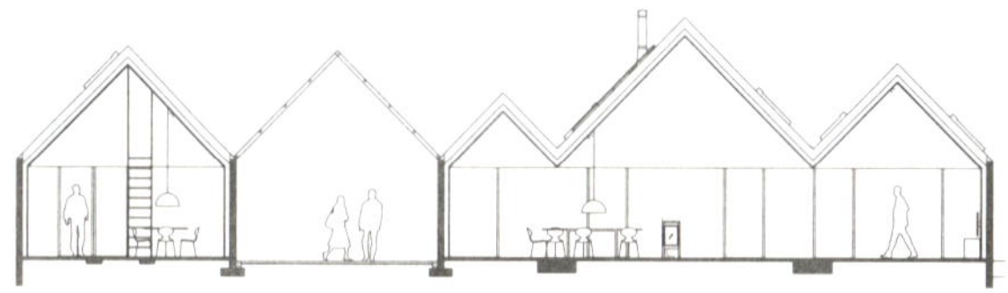
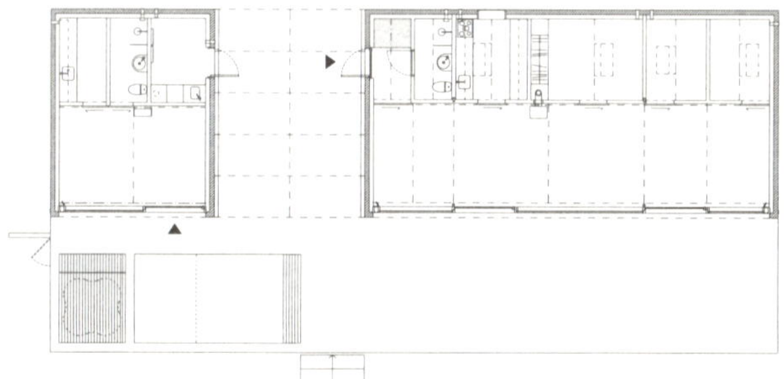

Terrace, interior floors and façades are made of exposed natural colored in-situ cast concrete with plywood formwork. The interior is painted white with woodwork in ash.

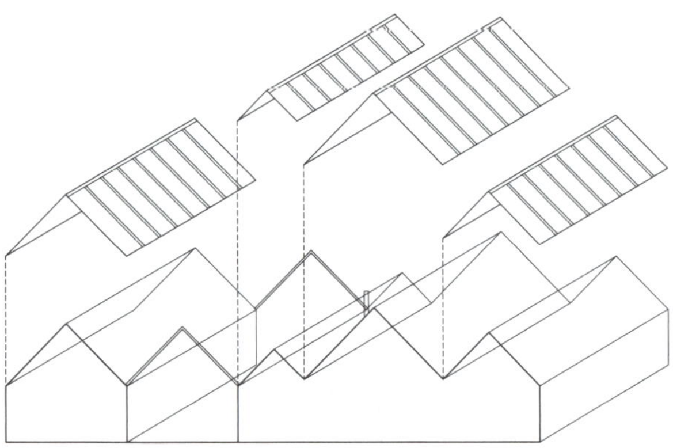

SINT JANSKLOOSTER

A spectacle of old and new stairs rewards you with a beautiful view after you have completed the 'route architecturale'.

Architects | Zecc Architects
Location | Barsbeek 6, Overijssel, The Netherlands
Completion | 1932 / 2014
Size | 330 sqm
Original use | water tower

The water tower is a historical landmark in the landscape of De Wieden, The Netherlands. This iconic building has now been made accessible for the public. It became a viewing tower, the 'route architecturale', which the new windows overlooking the surroundings reinforce even more. The connection among the people, landscape and the monumental water tower reinforces a feeling of identity with the place. The four new windows in the top provide a remarkable 360 degree view of the historical landscape. The building core is a 24-meter-high space housing an existing monumental stair and a new wooden sculptural stair. The new stairs form a contrast with the concrete walls of the tower. By adding the new route to the old existing one, spatial interaction is created. Where the old stairs followed the walls, the new stairs zigzag across the tower to reinforce spatial perception. The new stairs lead up to the level of the floor just below the immense concrete reservoir at a height of 28 meters.

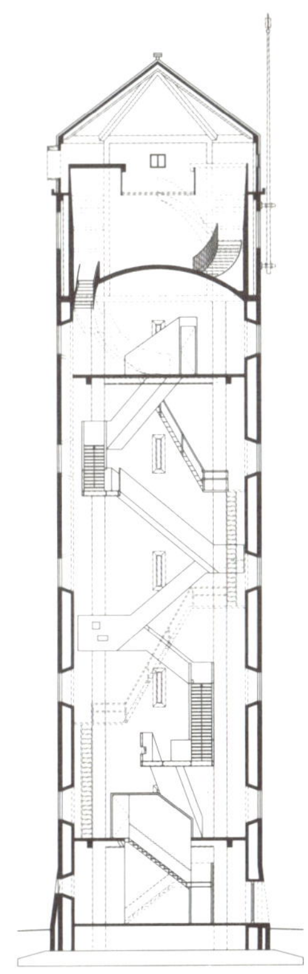

ANTOINE

Living with the Alps – a reverential tribute to art and simplicity in one.

Architects | BUREAU A
Location | Verbier, Switzerland
Completion | 2014
Size | 4 sqm

ANTOINE is a tribute to the alpine experience and to the writer Charles-Ferdinand Ramuz. The one-man wooden cabin is hidden inside a projected concrete rock. Referring to the long lasting Swiss tradition of hidden bunkers, the project integrates the highly urbanized landscape of the Alps. The military architecture utilizing principles of camouflage, described by French philosopher Paul Virilio in 1975, has long fascinated architects. ANTOINE creates an alpine shelter, a precarious "existence minimum" somewhat subversive in its use where one can freely enter and hide. It contains the very basic architectural elements - fireplace, bed, table, stool, window - but requires some risk taking on the part of the visitor because the rock is literally suspended in the field.

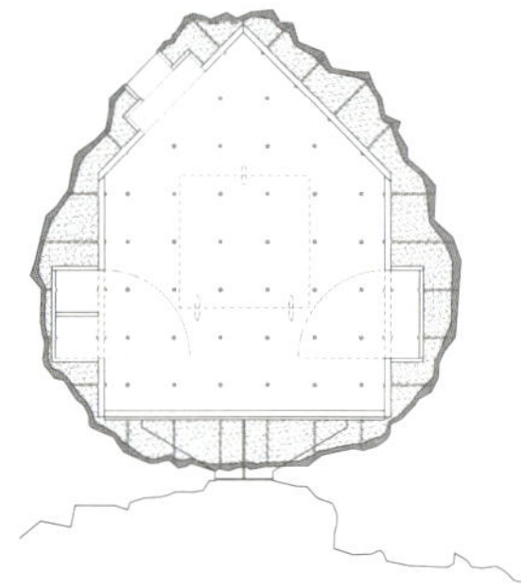

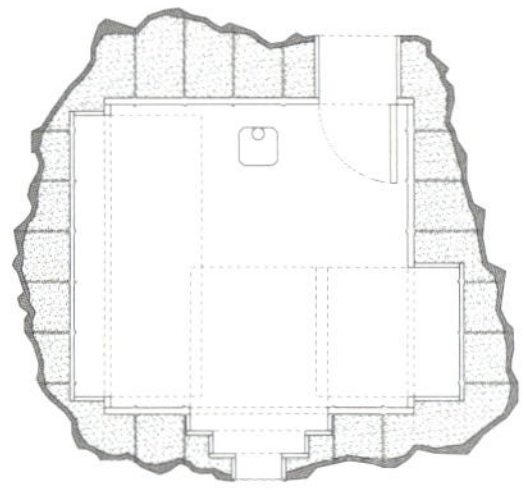

ANTOINE was commissioned by the artist residency Verbier 3d Foundation. It was self-built in the village and transported to the high-altitude sculpture park. The six weeks residency allowed for the construction of what can be considered an inhabited sculpture that follows the tradition of architecture-sculpture described by artist André Bloc and developed physically by André Bloc and Claude Parent.

MAV

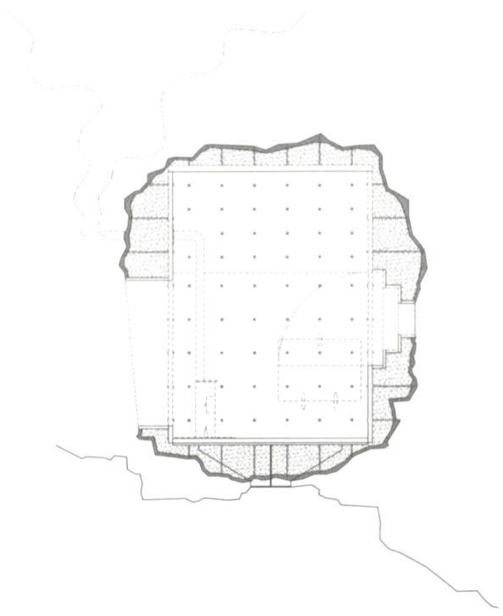

MARACANÃ HOUSE

Maracanã is in the hood. A continuous space that always leads you somewhere else.

The process of creating this house was intense, due to the absence of the architect-client relationship. Since there was never a formula for making family housing, creating it became a process of architectural research. Located on a lower level of the street, the site concept required increasing the volume to shelter the private area. The double height made a division between the social and private areas possible. The access floor features a transition area between the entrance to the house and what can happen after wandering through the space. It is space that allows the comprehension of the whole site and all its possibilities.

Architects | Terra e Tuma Associated Architects
Location | Rua Maracanã, São Paulo, Brazil
Completion | 2011
Size | 185 sqm

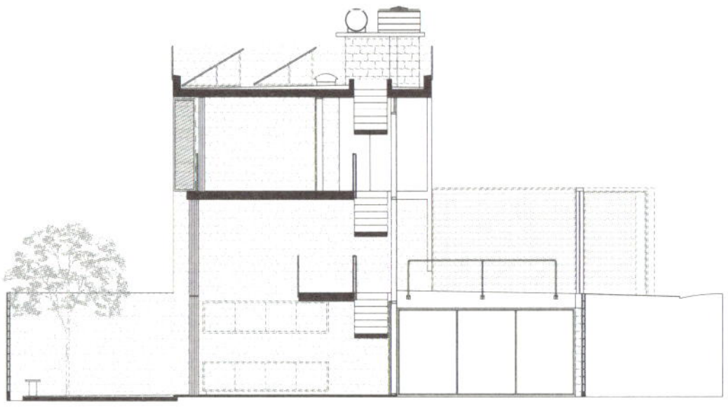

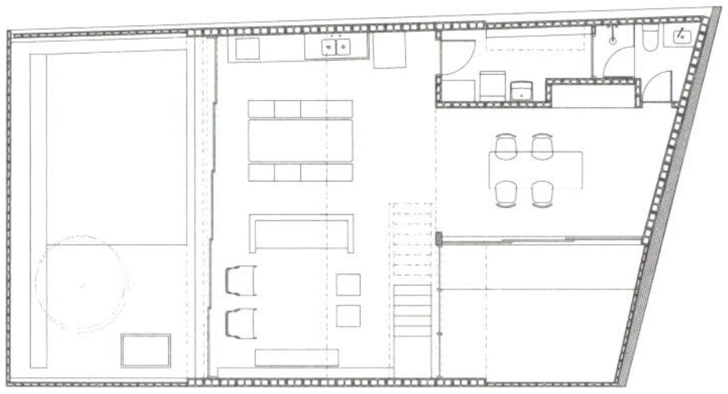

The initial condition of the house was defined by the site. The architects tried to take advantage of the difficulties of the site, to bridge gaps and to anchor the house firmly to the floor, which became the guiding principle of the project.

COMMUNITY CHURCH KNARVIK

Lots of wood and a shape referring to the fjords reveal the church's origin: in Norway, of course!

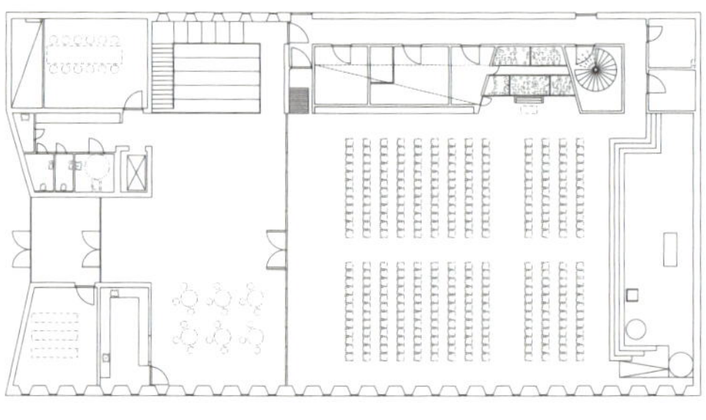

52

Architects | Reiulf Ramstad Arkitekter AS
Location | Knarvik, Hordaland, Norway
Completion | 2014
Size | 2,250 sqm

The new Community Church in Knarvik, located on the scenic west coast of Norway north of Bergen, is built on a privileged site overlooking the cultural landscape and local town center. The church signals its function with a sacral dignity and recognizable form, whereby the church spire, sanctuary and chapel are emphasized by ascending roof planes. Inspired by the local tradition of Norwegian stave churches, the building utilizes clear and elemental geometries, material and construction. The compact building volume is split into two stories on a rectangular plan, separating the sacred spaces above from the cultural and administrative functions below. An internal 'church square' connects the two levels with an atrium stair in a continuous space which may be joined or separated from the sanctuary with sliding glass walls to accommodate more than 500 people.

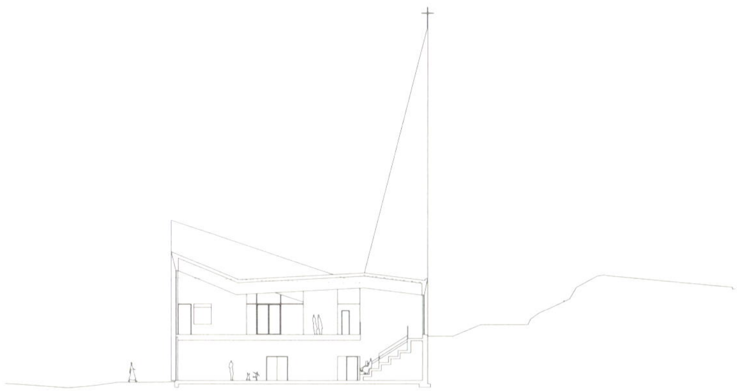

Wood is the key material of this project, expressed in the homogeneous cladding of pre-weathered pine heartwood and mirrored by the light-colored pine finish on all interior surfaces. The building permits daylight into its volume through lancet-like tall and narrow windows, separated in the plan to maximize admittance and reduce glare. At night, the warm glow of the interior reveals the activities of its religious and cultural events.

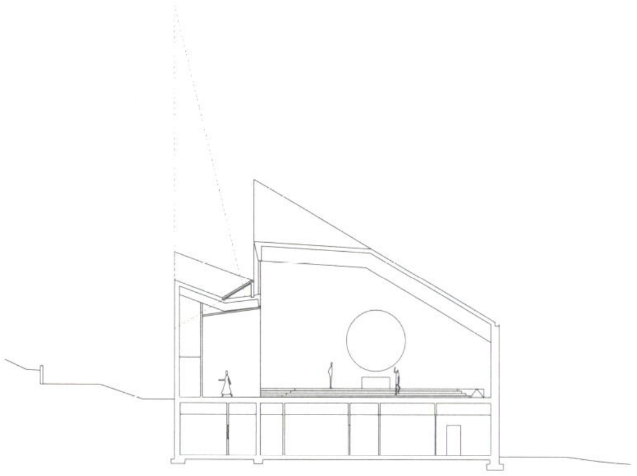

SCHREBER

Raw charm extended. The redefinition of mathematical equations.

Architects | AMUNT Architekten Martenson und Nagel Theissen
Location | Schreberstraße 6, 52070 Aachen, Germany
Completion | 1930 / 2011
Size | 144 sqm

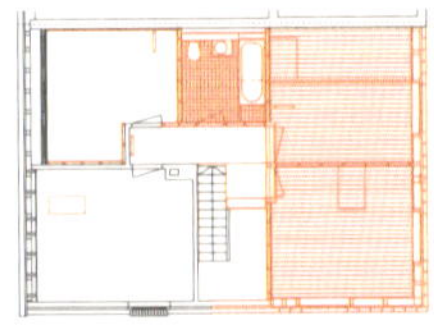

In the development of the Schreber project the architects carefully considered the existing stock in order to adapt it to modern conditions and the family's requirements. Instead of separating old and new, the emphasis was on building continuity. The annex expanded the house in the direction of the garden, creating striking rooms in the interior which form a unity with the existing stock. The dark red clinker façade of the original building meshes with the lightweight concrete pumice stone of the annex, contemporaneously interpreting the existing material and with its color combining it with the original building in a new, compact structure: 1+1=1. In the spirit of sustainability the repair principle was observed. Quality features, like existing floor coverings, windows or the wooden stairs were retained and extended.

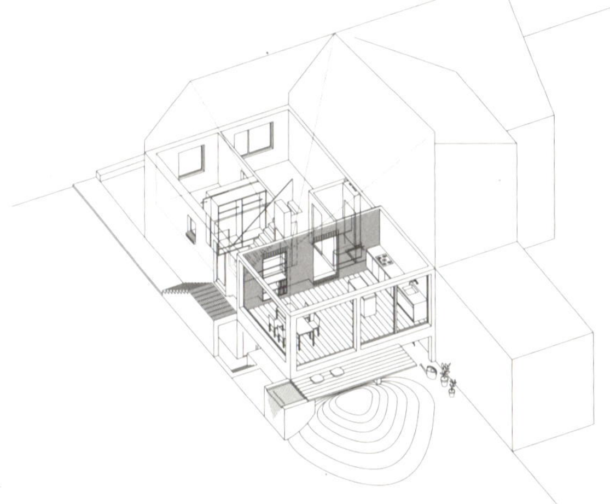

Instead of streamlined density, the architecture wants something special that breaks up perceptual spaces and traditional views and extends the raw charm of the former workers' settlement. The result is a marked contrast to the all too smooth perfection of the mainstream.

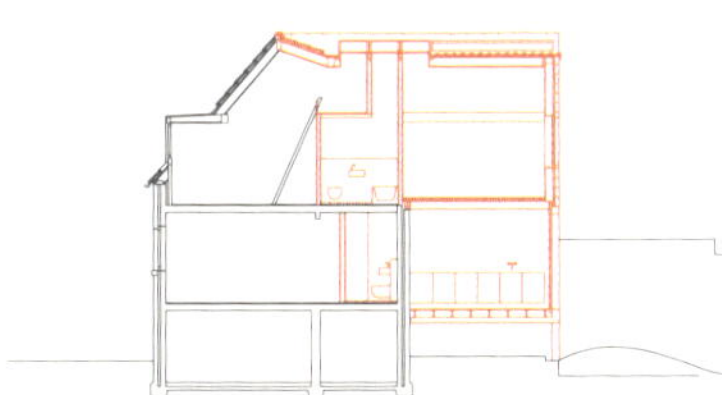

SOTOGRANDE'S SAILING SCHOOL

The stage is set perfectly: framed by the architecture, the sea and the Rock of Gibraltar become main characters of the space.

Architects | Héctor Fernández Elorza / HFE Arch., Carlos García Fernández
Location | Playa de los Catamaranes, San Roque, Cádiz, Spain
Completion | 2013
Size | 145 sqm

The sailing school for the Sotogrande's Royal Maritime Club is located between the marina and the catamaran beach. The project is linked to the stone jetty spanning longitudinally over the promenade on the north side of the beach. The structure seemingly levitates from the ground, standing gently in the sand, as if it too were a catamaran. Due to the limited dimensions of the school and its facilities it was deemed necessary to interpose a larger element to create more visibility for the building. The pergola, constructed in front of the school, unifies all the project elements while also creating a shaded threshold, shielding the exterior from direct sun exposure, stretching towards the southern end of the building. Seen from a distance, the school becomes a landmark near the port entrance.

The school is constructed with galvanized steel and bolted connections as the primary structure. The organization of the structural elements creates a series of rhythms in the façades emphasizing its nautical and weightless character.

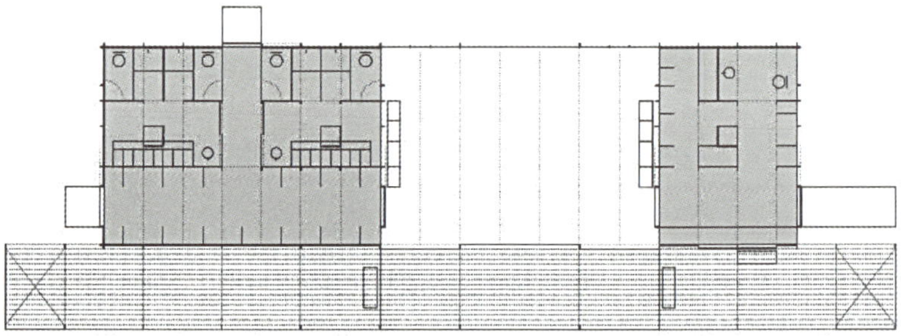

M4 FŐVÁM TÉR – UNDERGROUND STATION BUDAPEST

Like a public square ... but under ground and much more exciting!

Architects | sporaarchitects
Location | Fővám tér, Budapest, Hungary
Completion | 2014
Size | 3,000 sqm

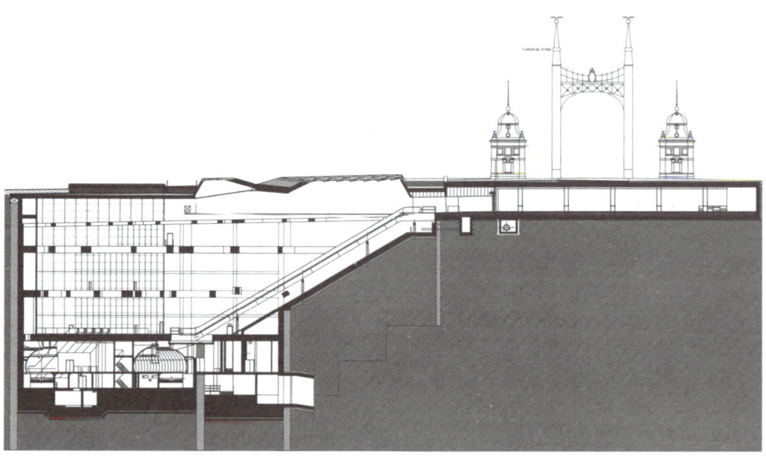

The new metro line planned in Budapest is to connect South-Buda with the city center. 10 stations are constructed in the first stage. The line is about 7 kilometers long. The main character of the stations is defined by the cut-and-cover technology, resulting in large underground boxes for the stations. The architectural decision was to clear these boxes, keeping only the necessary rough structures in the headspace of the stations. Thus huge reinforced concrete beams can be lit by natural light from above, creating an extraordinary effect in the deep stations.

Fővám tér station is one of the deepest stations of the line; it is situated below the bank of the Danube River on the Pest side, the surface area being part of the UNESCO World Heritage.

Fővám tér
Kijárat
Exit
Kijárat
Exit

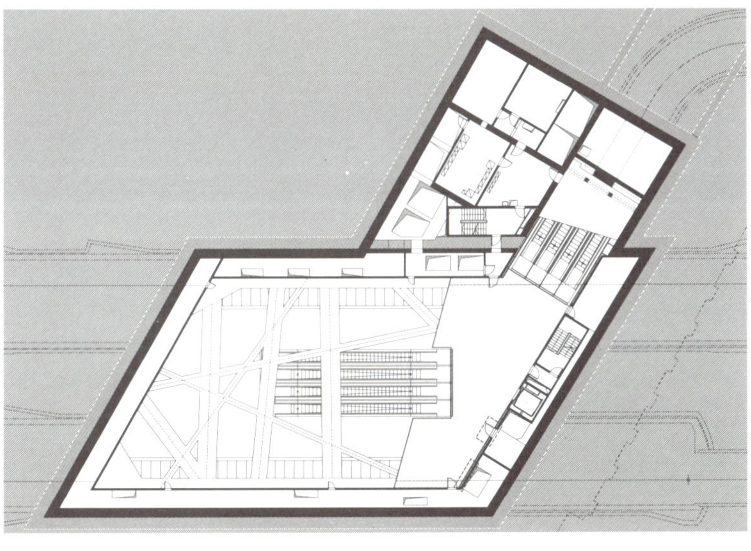

PATISSERIE À LA FOLIE

Probably the only place in the world where you're allowed to eat the artwork.

Architects | Atelier Moderno + Anne Sophie Goneau
Location | Montreal, Quebec, Canada
Completion | 2014
Size | 60.4 sqm

The design of the new address of the patisserie À La Folie aims to defy all stereotypes of the conventional pastry shop by giving full prominence to the superior presentation and quality of its unique products. The execution of the design begins with the storefront. The shop's 650 square feet ground floor location on the colorful street of Mont-Royal impelled the creation of a space that is distinguished by its neutrality, acting as a monochromatic backdrop to the vibrancy of both the street outside and the pastries within. The neutral gray interior elevates the wonderful shapes, textures, and hues of the products on display. This voluntary restraint isolates the senses, and the focus settles on the pastries themselves; the customer almost begins to taste with his eyes!

àlafolie
PÂTISSERIES AUDACIEUSES

All pastries are made in-house, with the production floor set in the rear of the space. It is separated from the shop area by a mid-height wall that encourages the sounds and smells of the kitchen to tease the senses of the patrons on the other side.

àlafolie
PÂTISSERIES AUDACIEUSES

àlafolie

Architects | Ricardo Carvalho + Joana Vilhena Arquitectos
Location | Rua Augusta 24, 1100-053 Lisbon, Portugal
Completion | 1952 / 2009
Size | 1,200 sqm
Original use | bank

The project for the Design and Fashion Museum (MUDE) provides an intervention at an old bank, initially designed by Cristino da Silva (1952). At the beginning of this decade the building was stripped of its original fittings. The project comprises an area to display the collection, temporary exhibitions, a bookshop, a café and an area for cultural events. The intervention in MUDE is primarily made with light, used to show the exposed concrete and the collection. The project is further characterized by the use of industrial materials: scaffolding canvas, pallets and reflective paint. The design and fashion items occupy the space in an informal way, establishing a close relationship with the visitor.

LISBON DESIGN AND FASHION MUSEUM

Restored by destruction. In the ruins of a Viennese-style building, MUDE found a lovely home.

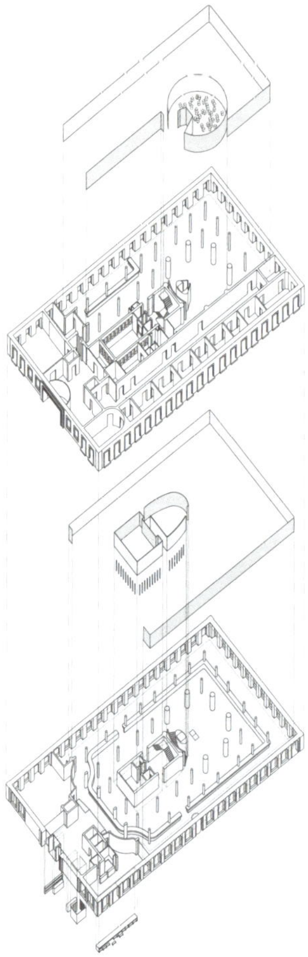

Ante-Estreia
Flashes do
Museu do Design
e da Moda

Architects | hda – Henrik Diemann Architekten
Location | Hammerbrookstraße 93, 20097 Hamburg, Germany
Completion | 2011
Size | 950 sqm
Original use | factory

The media agency Alphabeta is located in a former cooperative workshop, one of the few old buildings in the Hammerbrook quarter in Hamburg which was reconstructed after the bombings in 1943. The building is now listed. The spaciousness and the path of the incoming light lend the high, open space beneath the massive gabled roof a cathedral-like quality. In order to keep this special mood, architect Henrik Diemann decided to leave the existing construction as intact as possible. The ambience today is a blend of rough industry look and painted white chic. The raw surfaces of the iron and concrete skeleton, exposed cable ducts, large industrial lighting and uncovered Heraklith panels mounted beneath the ceiling emphasize the workshop character of the architecture. All constructive elements were spray-painted white. The magnesia flooring and the furniture designed by the architect have been painted white. The glowing green walls in the new access area provide a bright contrast.

ALPHABETA

Unlike the Greek alphabet, this is not confusing at all! A clear interior design mirroring a clear company concept of good work and efficiency.

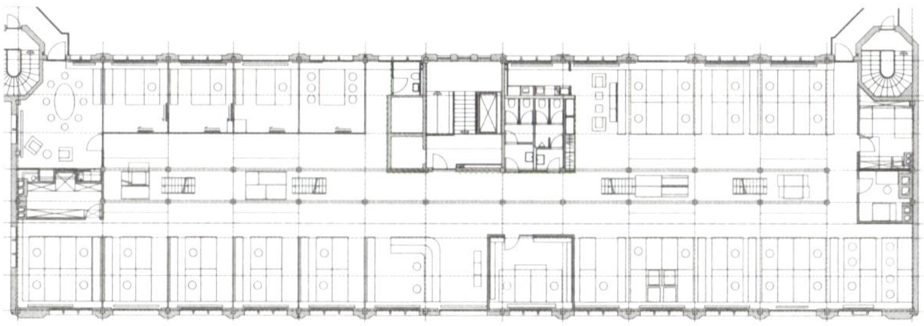

Four plateaus remain from a gallery which originally ran beneath the length of the roof ridge. They serve as free-standing conference islands for the Alphabeta media agency, and, with their massive supports, spatially integrate the large interior.

SEASONLESS HOUSE

Fantastic plastic. Bringing together urban landscape in one house.

Architects | Casos de Casas – Irene Castrillo Carreira and Mauro Gil-Fournier Esquerra
Location | Vinaroz, Castellón, Spain
Completion | 2013
Size | 361 sqm

The house combines a particular form of urban planning that is taking place in Vinaroz, and in some places on the coast of Castellón. According to the architects, typical housing blocks crowd the city center while the dedicated hot-season housing of locals and tourists is sited on the hillside, presenting a city with two opposing infrastructures. The Seasonless House distances itself from this way of living to create its own environment, which is domestic, adaptable and resilient for all seasons of the year with its own personal climate, for each inhabitant. A house without an exterior, because everything external can happen inside. The building is based on a standardized and modulated construction system personalized for specific needs.

Seasonless House is built from inside out, with double walls made from cellular polycarbonate, simple filters of undulated polycarbonate, interlocked metallic tiles, different types of glass according to the prevailing climate on either of its sides. The agro-textiles dissipate or accumulate the radiation. A house which is open and closed at the same time.

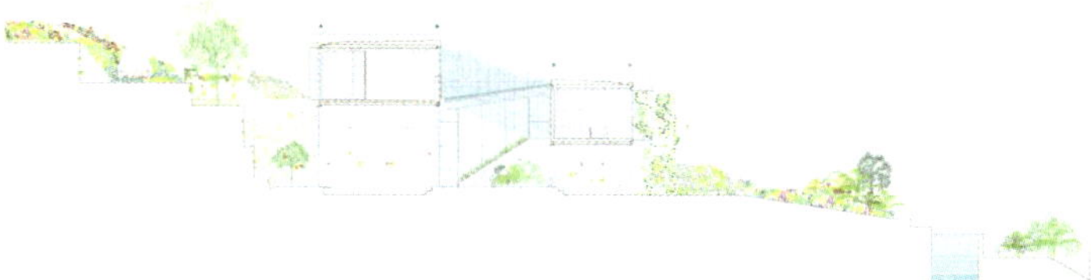

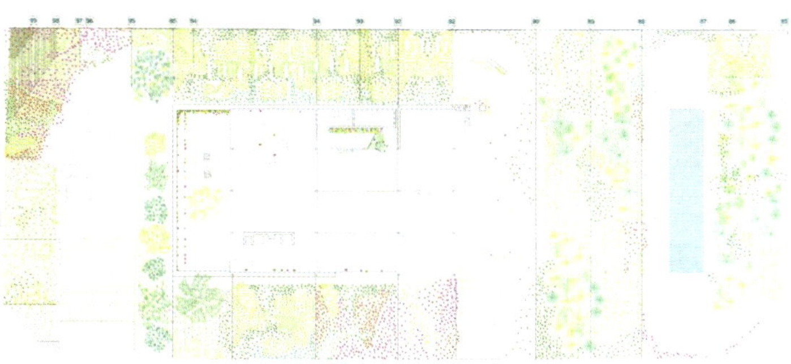

Z GALLERY

Welcome to the box. A dialogue between past and present, industry and art.

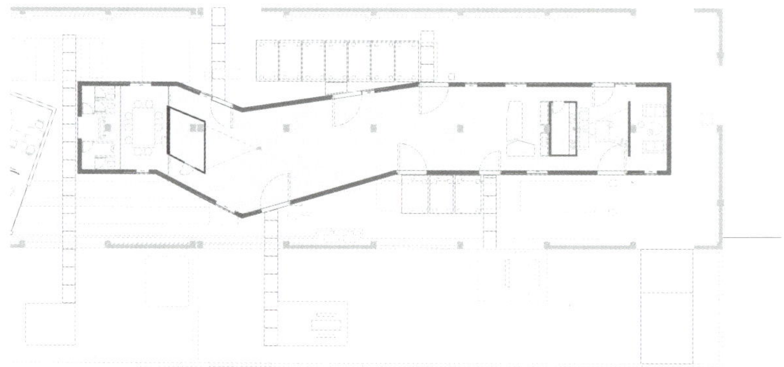

Architects | O-office Architects
Location | Kuipeng Road, Shenzhen, China
Completion | 1989 / 2013
Size | 2,963 sqm
Original use | workshop building for cloth purification

Z Gallery transformed the vacant former workshop building into a reception center for the new art area. The new building was conceived as a linear black steel box floating over the ruins. Exhibition, café, meeting rooms and a small reception area are fitted into the box. In order to respond to the summer heat and humidity of South China, the black box's façade is composed of a series of rotating and sliding glass walls and doors. They can facilitate different spatial usages for different events in different seasons, while reducing the energy cost for air conditioning. Seven independent gray boxes housing individual artist studios were located in Z Gallery, extending the spatial creation into the post-industrial ruins and zigzagging in-between the abandoned machine substrates.

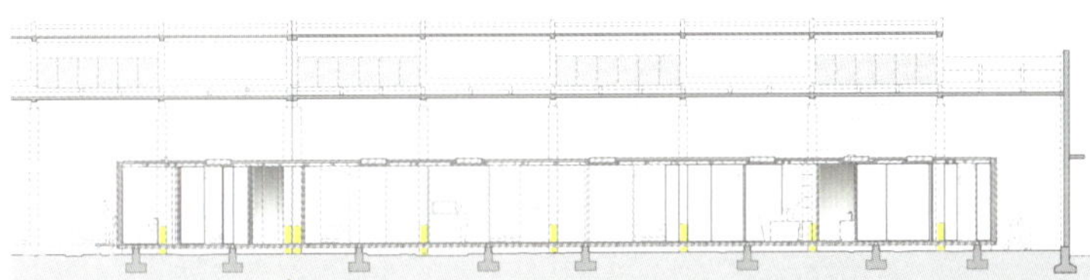

Z Gallery project is a perfect start and example of a new attitude in restoration and reusing industrial heritage. It tries to understand the old building and its spirit. The design process is based on the analysis of the existing state and heritage of the building. The new intervention follows the original spatial logic while rediscovering and highlighting the spatial potential of the old industrial location as a new cultural and commercial incubator.

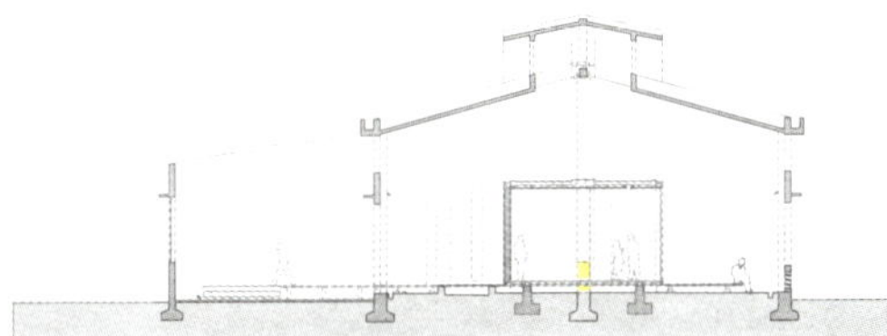

BRICK HOUSE

What if a house can last at least five generations instead of two? If made out of clay, your home's life expectancy could be 150 years!

Brick House is a vision of a house that is alive and can breathe. This vision is realized by reducing the complexity of the wall construction to one material, namely clay. By alternating clay blocks and standard bricks a simple, solid and homogeneous outer wall is created. This outer wall is diffusion-open thus allowing the building to breathe. The solid brick walls result in a robust and healthy house with a long lifespan, good indoor climate and low maintenance. Outside the house is basic, almost austere. But a more expressive double high interior, with exposed clay brick walls along with steel rods and wooden collar beams of the roof construction is exposed under the steep tiled roof. The ceilings feature unfinished plywood paneling. Special designed built-in furnishings made by LETH & GORI from mdf-board are finished with linoleum.

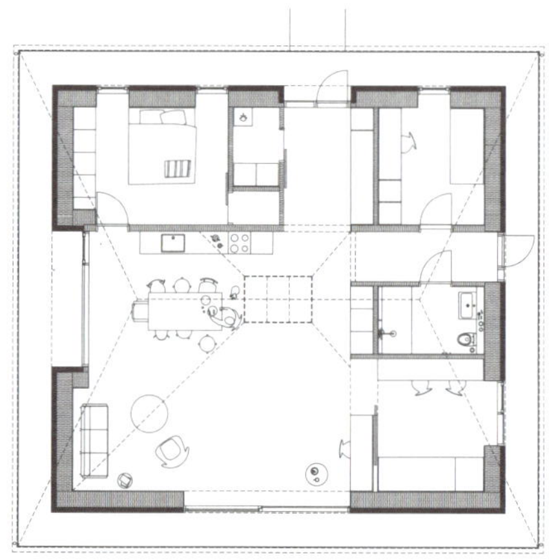

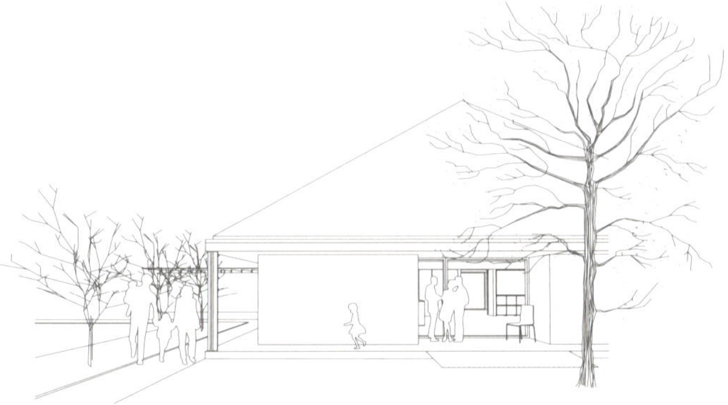

Architects | LETH & GORI
Location | Nyborg, Denmark
Completion | 2013
Size | 136 sqm

Innovation by reinventing history: revisiting materials and solutions from historic houses which have endured creates a new type of contemporary sustainable housing. Brick House has two main objectives: to create a house which is maintenance free for 50 years; and to create a house with a life span of a minimum of 150 years. The house is one of six "Mini-CO2 Houses", a project initiated by the Danish philanthropic foundation Realdania.

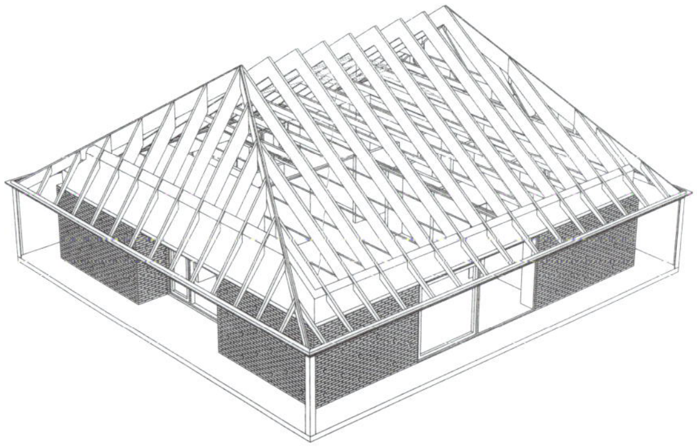

T HOUSE

T stands for terrific! Accurate planning results in a house with a spine.

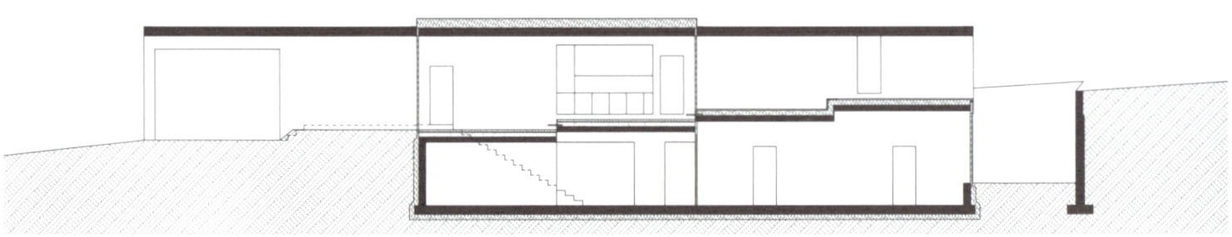

Architects | maria flöckner and hermann schnöll
Location | Tiefenbach, 5300 Hallwang, Austria
Completion | 2011
Size | 210 sqm

The backbone of the almost 30-meter-long house is formed by a central, one-meter-wide, mid-wall zone made of in-situ concrete. It accommodates all the side rooms, creating equivalent open or glazed room sequences on the north and south sides. The roof plate, also made of in-situ concrete, is a striking canopy jutting out over a two-story spatial structure. This structure comprises two thirds of the length of the house and is half buried in the ground. Eight landings, offset to each other by two steps, follow the course of the slope, so that each landscaped level merges smoothly with the topography. And by the way, Tiefenbach is part of the Fischachtal, not far from the city of Salzburg.

One structure with two atmospheres. Open, free living outside and sheltered, stable living inside. Above ground one could speak of 'living outdoors' within the glazed climate skin beneath the roof umbrella. Living quarters underground are in the climate controlled body of earth in the recessed garden courtyard. Room uses above and below ground are interchangeable. Both situations contribute to the whole and create a range of perception for the inhabitants far beyond the building structure.

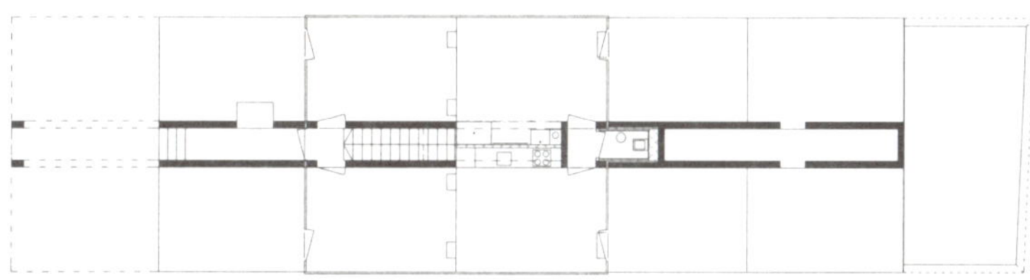

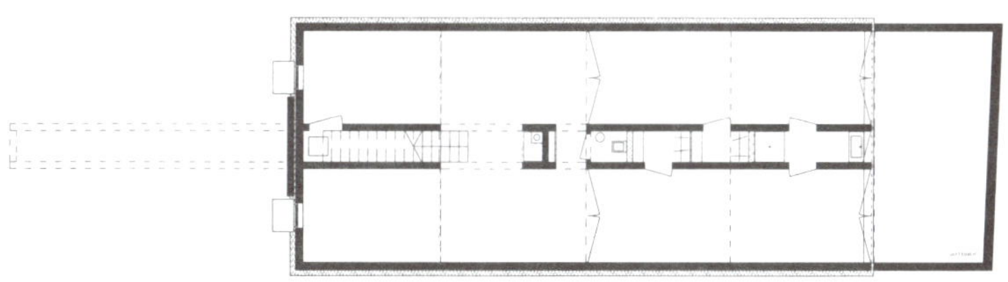

In the city of Cluny, the surrounding wall of Cluny Abbey is a piece of scenery, undisturbed in the sweep of history. Its shape doesn't seem to call for any change. In one of the most protected areas of the city, the new use permitted graft on a new component. The restaurant is set on the triangular remains of a ruined building that specifies its own volumetric wrapping. The bulk of the project is based on the use of the very close surroundings that combine the fortifications (partially hidden by the ruin), the narrow Buteveaux Tower and the discreet Medasson River. The plans underscore the strong and dominant parts of the site. Two different types of spaces are in the restaurant: the kitchen and reception and the cafeteria.

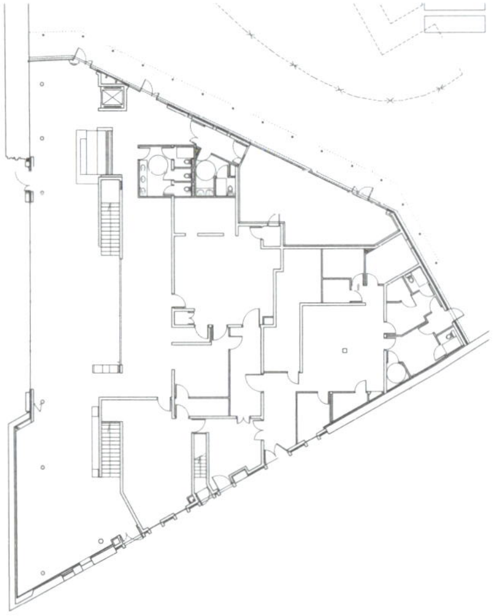

L'ENSAM DE CLUNY RESTORATION / ABBAYE DE CLUNY

Transplant successfully completed. Thanks to the use of weathered steel, the addition fits perfectly in the medieval environs.

Architects | Bernard Desmoulin
Location | Abbaye de Cluny, Cluny (71) rue de Paris, France
Completion | 2009
Size | 1,500 sqm

Materials were chosen in tune with the site. They answer the need to distinguish them clearly but not in aggressive opposition. The materials convey an irremovable aspect to the building with a light texture touch (steel skins with patina and wood), that can be inserted into the medieval context. The association of these materials answers the sensibility of the place as much as its patrimonial quality.

RUE
PORTE
DE PARIS

WRITER'S SHED

A gingerbread house in the middle of London. There could be no better inspiration for writing great children's literature.

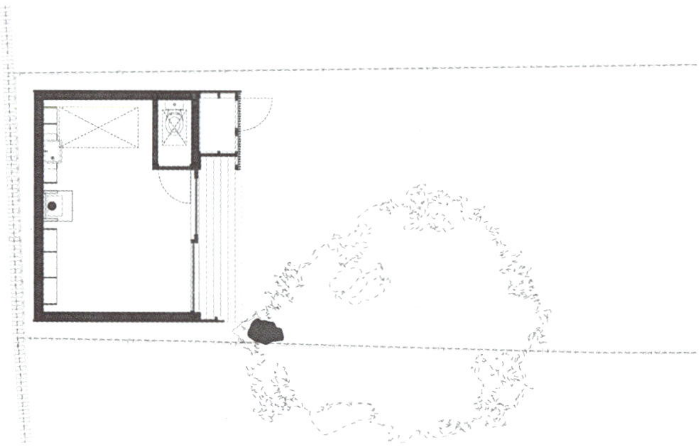

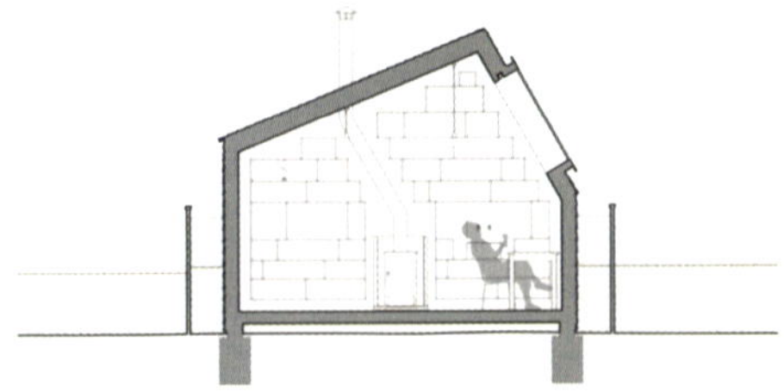

Architects | Weston Surman & Deane Architecture
Location | Hackney, London
Completion | 2013

WSD Architecture were commissioned by an author and illustrator to design and build a writer's shed. Capitalizing on their multi-disciplinary backgrounds, WSD acted as designers, project managers, and lead contractors. The design responds to the client's passion for children's literature and mythologies. The space is conceived as a haven in the city; a fairy-tale hut at the bottom of the garden where the client can retreat and immerse himself in his work. Externally, the glowing cedar façade, shingle cladding, and chimney all play a part in creating this world. Inside, a large north-facing skylight floods the workspace with natural light. On the gable wall, a bookcase meanders around the wood burning stove, providing a center piece for the client to store his library. Looking back out over the garden, the glazed sliding door opens up on a covered verandah – a perfect place to enjoy the very worst of the British weather.

The material palette is modest and unassuming, whilst also resilient and sensitive to ageing, complementing the role of the shed as a place of changing ideas and production. Oiled OSB and painted tongue and groove pine were used for the floors, walls and shelving, while utilitarian garden taps and brass splash-backs surround the reclaimed Belfast sink. A hearth made of cut concrete paving slabs was built to surround the stove.

HILARY MANTEL

WILDE

AUNTS AREN'T GENTLEMEN
P.G. WODEHOUSE
Leave It to Psmith
Life at Blandings

HOUSE C AND HOUSE D

No, this is not Japan ... The gabled roof volumes in sparkling steel may say Tokyo, but their shape and structure is 100% Serbian rural tradition.

House C and House D are a part of the "Terra Panonica" estate, a cultural and tourist complex for various creative and leisure activities, located in Mokrin, Serbia. House C and House D occupy the positions of free-standing utility structures of the former rural household and are focused on the central area of the property. In form, structure and material they invoke associations with the utility sheds of the contemporary local households which are essentially just parts of the courtyard covered by a steel canopy. In that sense, the interior of both houses is designed to evoke an impression of such a canopy rather than an enclosed interior space. This feature is further accentuated by the same material in the shell in the interior and on the façade.

Architects | studio AUTORI
Location | Svetog Save 25, Mokrin, Serbia
Completion | 2014
Size | 791 sqm

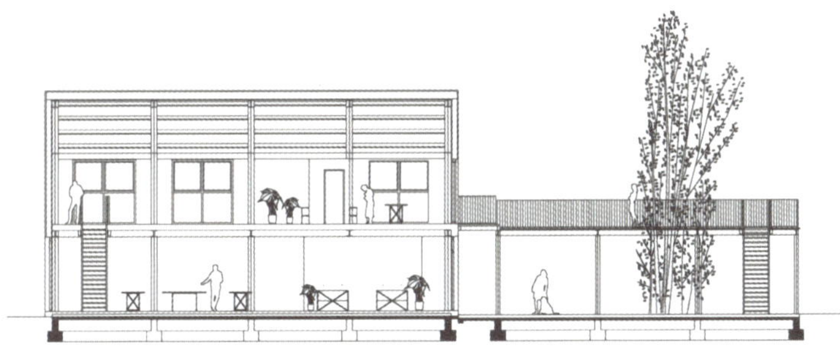

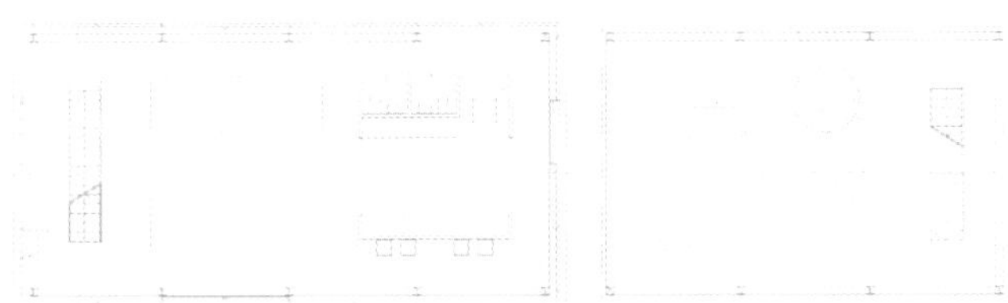

Since the complex was built on the site of the former rural estate the disposition, volume and shape of the new buildings have been determined by the original houses, while their functional relations adhere to the structural logic of the local rural households.

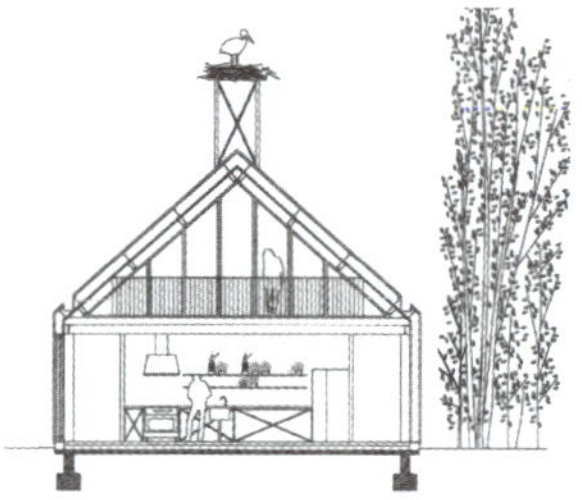

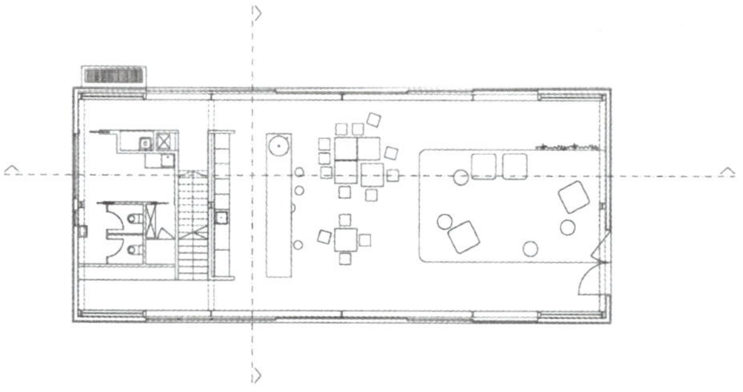

VISITOR AND INFORMATION CENTER SPARRENBURG

Transferring the language of the old into the new. This is architectural poetry expressed in tamped concrete.

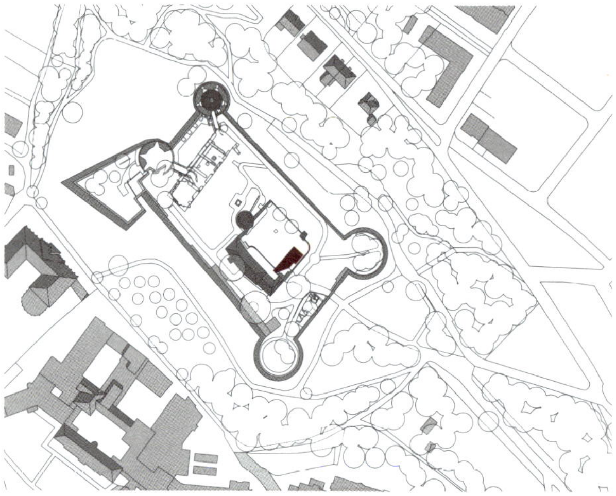

Architects | Max Dudler
Leading architect/project manager | Simone Boldrin
Co-workers | Kilian Teckemeier, Thomas Back
Construction supervision | Architektenbüro Stüwe, Bielefeld for Büro Max Dudler
Structural engineers | Prinz & Pott GmbH, Bielefeld
Location | Sparrenburg, Am Sparrenberg, 33602 Bielefeld, Germany
Completion | 2014
Size | 136 sqm
Original use | gate threshold of the castle courtyard

The one-story new Sparrenburg Visitors' Center is inserted as an independent building in the south-east side of the castle courtyard. Together with the gatehouse it forms a new entrance area which revives the historical gate threshold. At the same time the shape of the structure successfully encloses the castle courtyard. The intervention orients the sequence and arrangement of the outer rooms like a compass, improving the functional requirements of the current use of the castle as a monument and observation platform. The structure is monolithically stamped concrete. The colors and textures of the castle ruins merge with each other like the layers of sedimentary stone. The lively structure of the dry concrete and stamped layers is a visual testimony to the craftsmanship applied here.

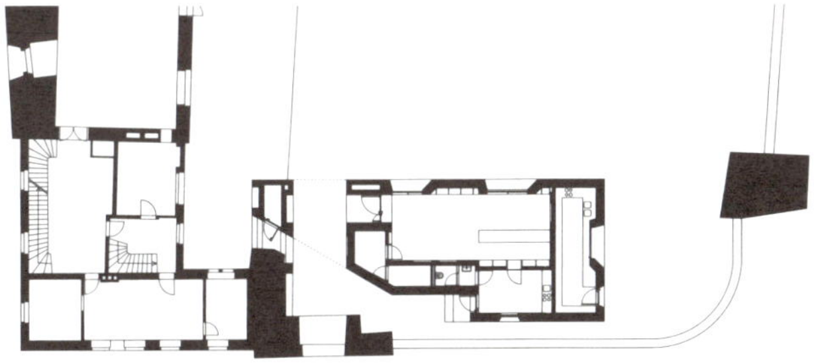

"Instead of a reconstruction of a certain historical state the architecture is a contemporary layer inserted in the changeful history of the town. It maintains an existence independent of construction phases and styles, favoring neither the medieval castle, the recent fortress, the 19th century reconstruction nor the destruction of World War II. The architecture expresses the existing substance." Max Dudler

HOUSE 1014

Brick is Beautiful – in all its shapes and sizes.

The desire of the owners was to differentiate two zones in the house. The orientation of the plot and its narrowness made it difficult to achieve good solar gain throughout the street façades. This fact, added to the difficulties to achieve privacy in the ground floor, led the architects to move back the building from the front street line, creating access patios on both sides of the house. These bioclimatic spaces become the first step in a sequence of areas linking one street to the other. The organization, based on sequenced spaces, is totally related to the structural system of the house, involving a wall system. Load bearing walls are stratified to create a gradient of different densities. Material and spatial distribution contribute to the passive behavior of the house.

Architects | HARQUITECTES (David Lorente, Josep Ricart, Xavier Ros, Roger Tudó)
Location | Granollers, Barcelona, Spain
Completion | 2014
Size | 673 sqm

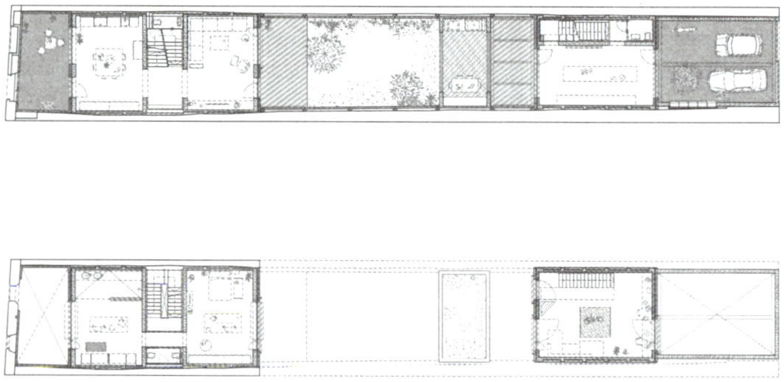

50

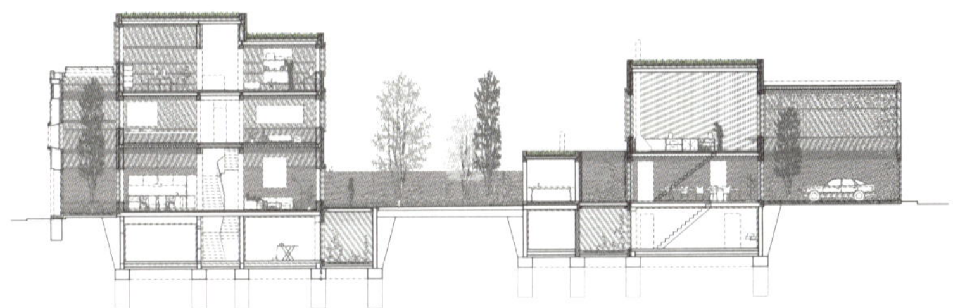

CHAMELEON HOUSE

A chameleon's-eye view for your very own orchard in every room.

Architects | Petr Hájek ARCHITEKTI
Location | Prague - Lipence, Czech Republic
Completion | 2013
Size | 137 sqm

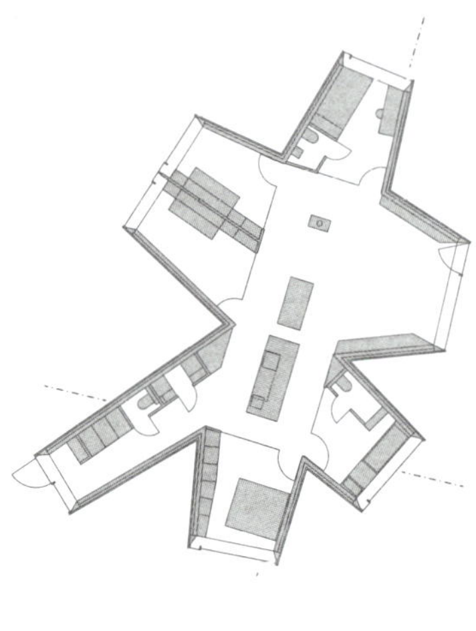

The inspiration for this house is a chameleon resting in the meadow. Eyes (windows) unrestrictedly observe the surroundings. The skin (façade), consisting of a semi-gloss coat, partly reflecting the colors of the garden and the sky. Each single room is oriented to one of the trees. The living room faces the apple tree, the master bedroom, the cherry tree, the bathroom faces the peach tree, the guest room, the silver spruce and the children's room, the walnut. The geometry of the concrete walls creates two different types of spaces on one plot: "The house spaces" are facing the trees in the garden, whereas the "garden spaces" are intervals between "the house spaces", since they are in fact invisible from the interior.

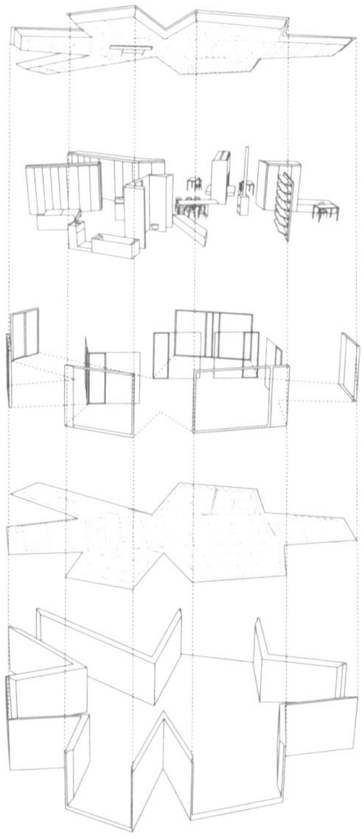

Floors and inner partitions consist of beech veneered timber. The formwork pattern of the concrete ceiling is mirrored in the pattern of the floor plates.

Architects | group8
Location | Chemin Philibert de Sauvage 37, 1219 Châtelaine, Geneva, Switzerland
Completion | 2010
Size | 820 sqm
Original use | factory

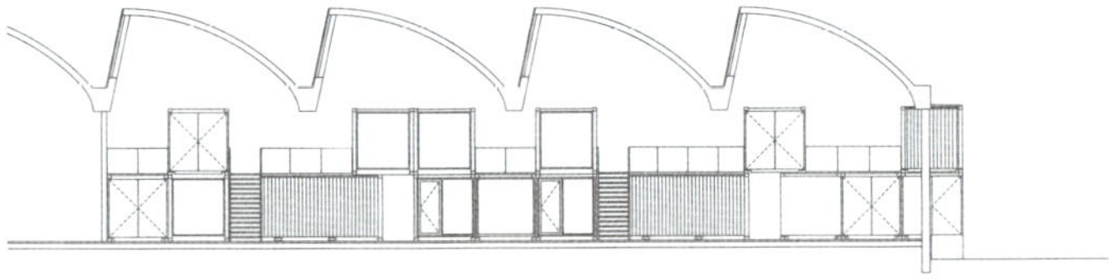

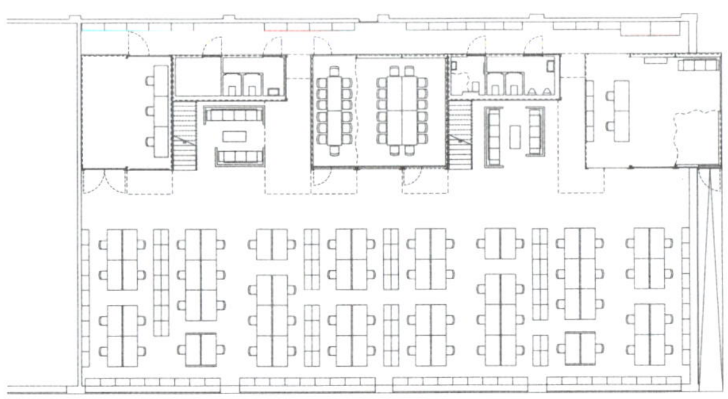

CARGO

More than just a pretty face ... 16 retired containers are the centerpiece of this modern office solution.

The Cargo project involves the renovation of a former industrial hall converted into group8's offices. A bright space contains a hidden treasure: recycled shipping containers. Following Marcel Duchamp's idea of ready-made, these monumental objects acquire a new function, embodying a collective form or a situation of the architects' work, like a model workshop, cafeteria or sanitation. The other half of the scheme is in opposition to the containers' structured zone: a white and luminous open space which generates a strong synergy of work and gives shape to a neutral environment favoring creativity.

HANJIN

HDMU
217164
KR 2210
HYUNDAI

EVERGREEN
HYUNDAI
TARE
NET
CU.CAP.

HJCU 894469 5
RGREEN

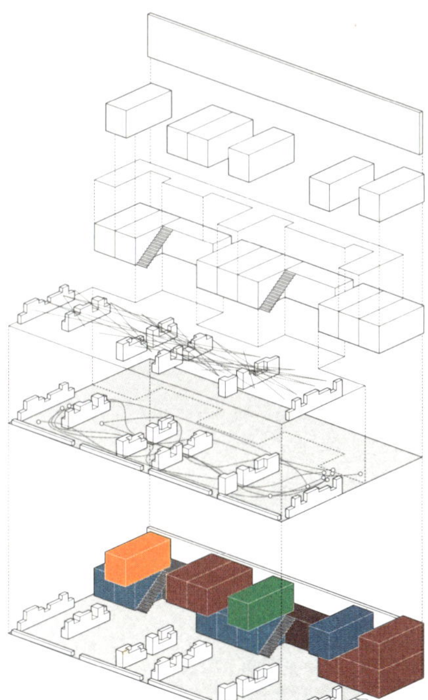

Architects | raumhochrosen – Heike Schlauch and Robert Fabach
Location | Vienna Woods, Austria
Completion | 2012
Size | 28.5 sqm

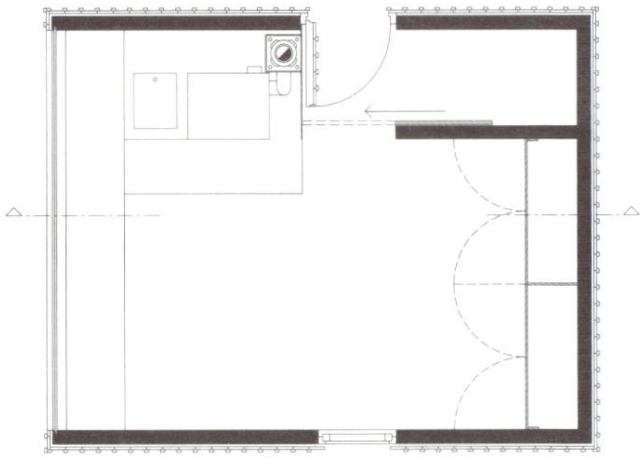

TOM'S HUT

Withdrawing from the countless bright and glittering things of the day-to-day world to a place with just a few archaic, natural elements which promise adventure.

A corporate coach who is also an Austrian singer-songwriter and lives in two worlds needs a location with some wilderness and a hut off the beaten path as a counterbalance to life in the city. This simple house has strong ties to its surroundings, following the contour of a predecessor building that had collapsed. It was literally designed around a human being and his passions. Life in his retreat is contained in an angular space on two levels. Enclosed on all sides with shutters, the hut can be opened up to different views. The prefabricated wood structure contains all the necessities in compact quarters. A striking architectural identify becomes a location for retreat, hospitality and personal development.

Out of the city through the open fields into the forest. The footpath to the hut, stepping into the shelter. Warmth, cooking, sleep and return to oneself.

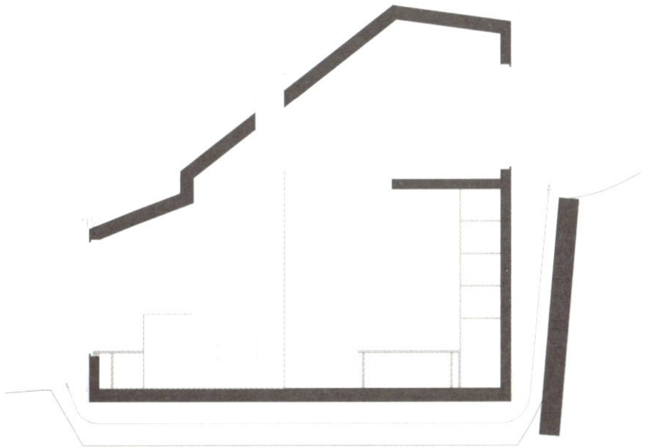

GREEN BOX

Green, green, green my clothes are all green; all that I have is green, green, green ... But my darling is not the hunter, it's this hideaway in the midst of nature.

Architects | act_romegialli
Landscape | Gheo Clavarino
Location | Cerido SO, Italy
Completion | 2011
Size | 40 sqm
Original use | small disused garage

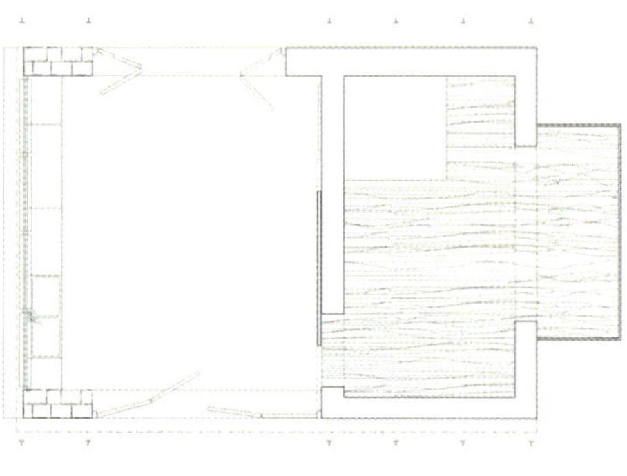

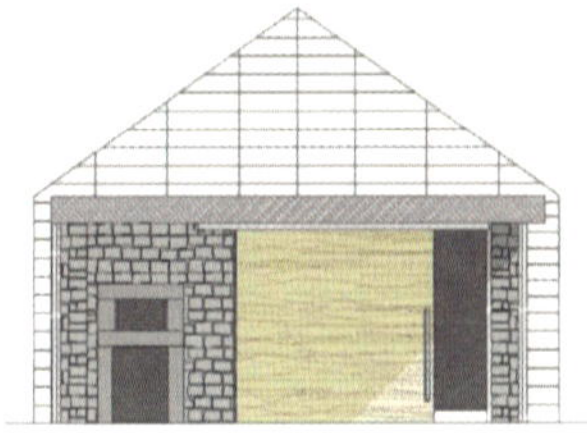

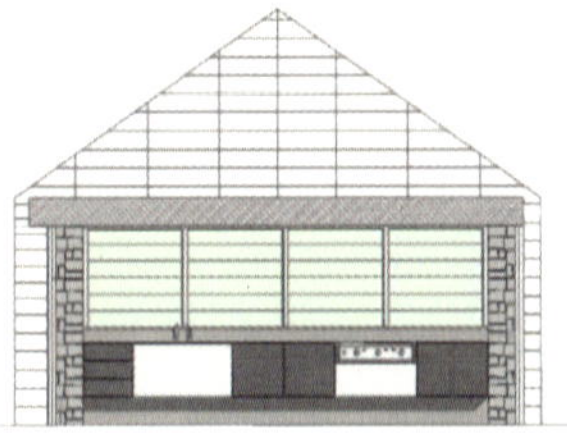

The Green Box project involves the renovation of a small disused garage appended to a weekend house on the slopes of the Raethian Alps. A structure of lightweight metal galvanized profiles and steel wires defines the volume as a three dimensional support for the climbing vegetation. The vegetation is mainly deciduous: Lonicera periclymenum and Polygonum baldshuanicum are the base for the secondary layer of Humulus lupulus and Clematis tangutica. On the basement level groups of herbaceous perennials alternate with annuals and bulbs to ensure a light but continuous flowering. There is a room inside the pavilion for the gardening tools (a great passion of the owner), an area for cooking and a space for conviviality. Green Box is a small green shelter in the vegetation, a privileged observation point of the changing of the seasons of the surrounding park.

Materials are rudimentary; galvanized steel for the kitchen, larch planks for flooring and big sliding doors, windows in unpainted galvanized steel, simple pipes for the water supply.

COMPACT KARST HOUSE

Stone meets concrete meets wood. Slovenia blossoms out to be the current architectural hotspot.

Architects | dekleva gregoric architects
Location | Vrhovlje 9C, 6221 Dutovlje, Slovenia
Completion | 2014
Size | 92 sqm

The design of the small compact stone house corresponds to the needs of the young family and simultaneously follows current technological principles and the tradition of small, compact, stone and almost windowless houses. The proto-house concept obtains clarity from the monolithic volume, with two inserted wooden proto-houses connected with the shared open gallery. The project poses the question about the characteristics of anonymous traditional built architecture from which it originates, establishing a relationship between contemporary interpretation and the traditionally conditional domain of synthesis.

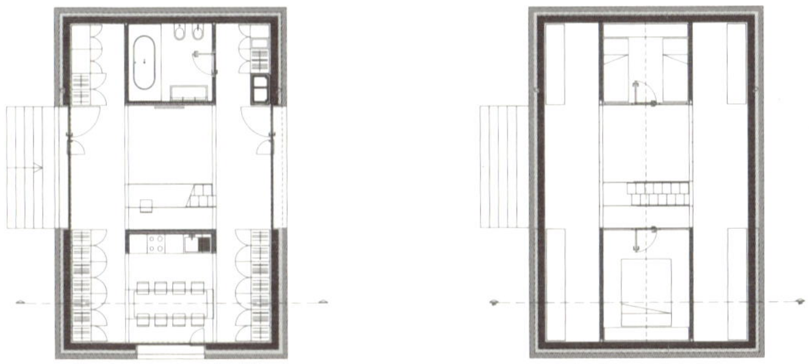

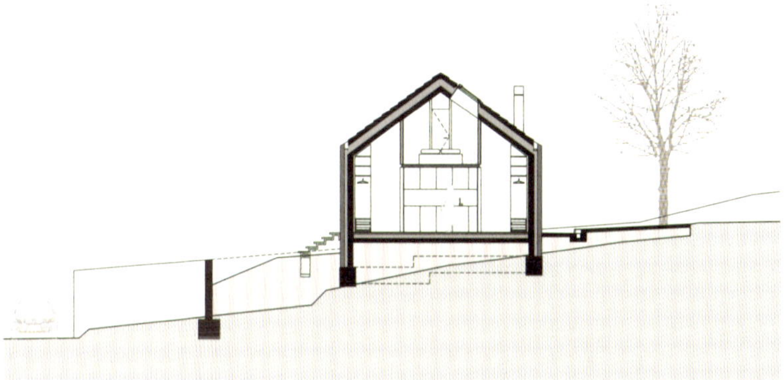

The redefinition of the traditional stone Karst roof, with its texture, color, material and its steep inclination, is executed as a contemporary concrete interpretation with considerable technological ingenuity. The inseparable connection between the façade and the roof is the key allusion to the image of a traditional Karst village. The local limestone, set into the concrete during the casting process, gives the walls the appearance of having a solid masonry construction.

NEW CHURCH ZIERIKZEE RENOVATION

Put on your best dress and get ready to walk down the red carpet. What glamour in such a venerable building!

Architects | GROUP A
Location | Kerkplein 1, Zierikzee, The Netherlands
Completion | 1848 / 2014
Size | 1,060 sqm
Original use | church

With a collection of clever, simple interventions the interior of the Nieuwe Kerk Zierikzee has been refurbished. GROUP A's design connects the church square with the interior through a 'red carpet' principle. Outside this has been realized by projecting images onto the square while inside a new poured epoxy resin floor runs all the way through the center of the interior. Inside, an elegant box, the Gallery, has been added, housing the ticket sale, rest rooms, bar, kitchen and storage space. A semi-concealed staircase in the Gallery leads visitors to an exclusive view onto the event floor and out through the high church windows. Two sets of transparent draught lobbies have been added to keep the imposing entrance doors hospitably open. Prior to refurbishment the monumental church building was restored.

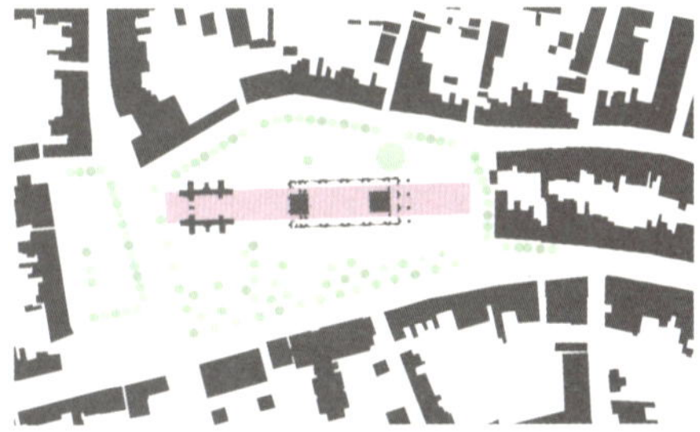

The new resin floor in the middle of the church makes room for the magnificent gravestones at the sides while providing the opportunity to install an efficient floor heating system. The low temperature floor heating system uses preheated air from under the dark slate roof where it is led through a heat exchanger to benefit from the heat already present in the attic. The 'red carpet' and the Gallery, both in the same color, form a strong new gesture without overpowering the monumental interior.

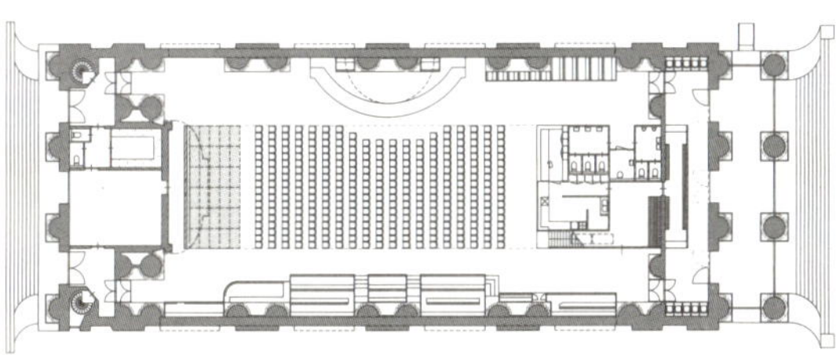

Architects | Atelier Data
Location | Varatojo, Torres Vedras, Portugal
Completion | 2013
Size | 380 sqm

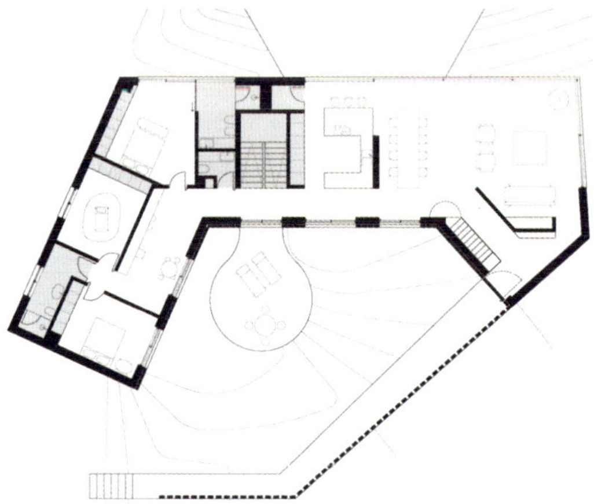

VARATOJO HOUSE

So much more than just a house. This is experimentalism with a view!

The Varatojo House is placed on a hill, east of the city of Torres Vedras, Portugal. Set on a polygonal plot with sun exposure (predominantly north/south) and a mainly northern wind direction, the design strategy began by considering the following issues: promoting relationship between building and landscape and taking advantage of the location's position overlooking the city, castle and surroundings. Other issues were encouraging a strong complementarity between the house and the garden in order to create an intense visual relationship between the inside and the outside, between construction and natural elements, creating transversal relations between the north side (view) and the south side (inner garden) mainly through the pool on the lower level and the garden landscape. The use of recycling materials such as the wooden pilings from the walls of the former railway sleepers, introducing a certain experimentalism and innovation which is different from the way the material is usually used and encouraging the use of native plants in the garden were also factors.

The house is shaped by a spiral gesture intending to take advantage of the plot outline. This gesture starts with the ramped access to the lot and ends on the opposite side of the house, reaching here two-stories high, so that the contour of the house also reinforced this spiral gesture. The design strategy adopted created a living space on the site's south side, protected from the strong northern winds, which determined the main construction on the north side.

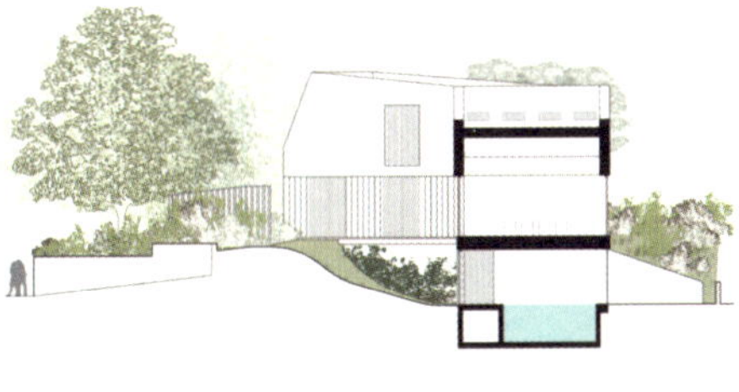

CASA CAJA – BOX HOUSE

Big bang for the bucks! S-AR's contribution to affordable but well-designed housing.

Architects | S-AR
Location | Zuazua, Nuevo Leon, Mexico
Completion | 2014
Size | 110 sqm

This project tries to create a competitive and viable house typology for low to middle income families. The house is defined like a box containing other boxes inside. The first box is placed in the middle of the plot, with one side left open. This generates a side yard that brings natural lighting and ventilation into the house. At the same time this free space can be used for social activities defined by the first floor of the house. On the second floor there is a private area, one side of which can be opened with doors in order to allow the users to regulate their privacy, lighting and ventilation in the rooms. Across from this area is a more open enclosure in the lower level linked with the side yard.

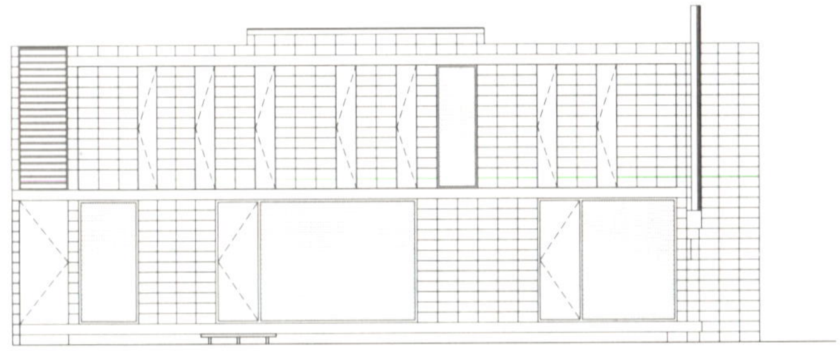

As a social architecture project, the construction methodology assumes active participation of the future users. This is a way for them to strike roots, with a responsibility for the development of the project. The family, co-workers, relatives and friends contribute to the process week by week. The costs are thereby reduced significantly and the value of family teamwork is enhanced. Construction as a didactic process.

Architects | Petr Hájek ARCHITEKTI
Location | Dobrovského 3, Vrchlabí, Czech Republic
Completion | 2014
Size | 962 sqm

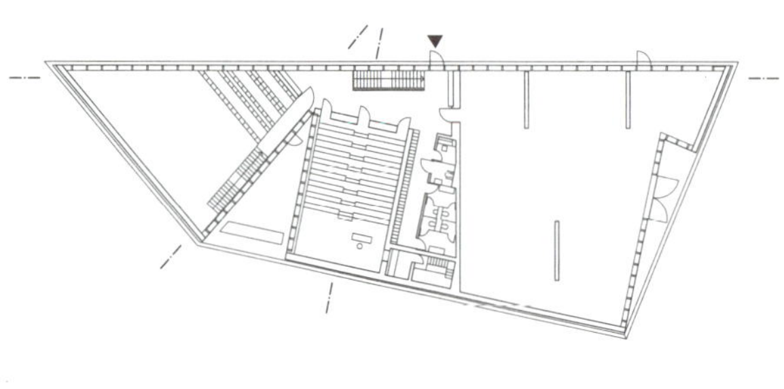

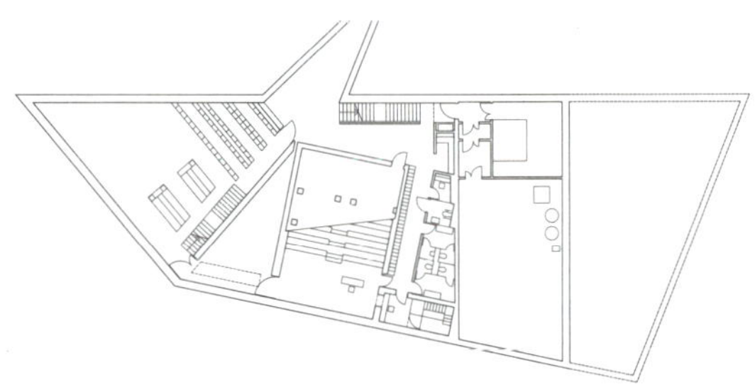

KRKONOSE MOUNTAINS CENTRE FOR ENVIRONMENTAL EDUCATION (KCEV)

Copy and paste. For the architecture, there was no better inspiration than that offered by the beautiful landscape.

KCEV was intended to become a place for environmental education, the organization of public lectures, international conferences and research projects. The building is situated in the castle park close to the central office building of the Krkonoše Mountains National Park. The ambience of the public space between the existing building and the new center is emphasized by a glazed wall, which conveys the inner life to pedestrians. The object is a hybrid between a building and the landscape. The geometry of the object refers to the geometry of the Krkonoše Mountains - each single slope has its natural counterpart. The roof is not some minimized cut-out, but contains information about the formation of the Krkonoše Mountains. The exterior is designed like a "mountain meadow", whereas the inner ceiling consists of smooth, exposed concrete, symbolizing the rocks. Inner partitions and furniture are made of timber. The building itself is energy efficient with a minimum of heat loss and is heated with a heat pump.

7

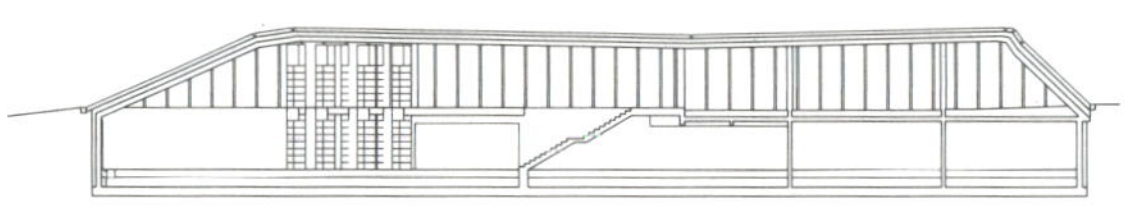

BLACK WOOD HOUSE

Where does the house end and where the forest start?

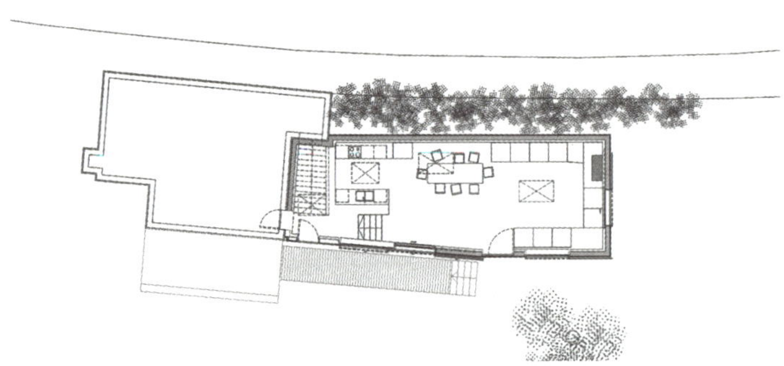

Architects | Marchi Architectes
Location | Les Petites Dalles, Normandy, France
Completion | 2012
Size | 80 sqm

The client wanted to move the living spaces to a more open and transparent area in order to free some spaces in the old house. A unique volume is set up involving the kitchen, living and dining rooms. There are broad views of the garden and landscape from the interior. The extension is connected to the existing house as a structurally light volume, in order not to overload the foundations. The project is minimal: the volume is integrated in the surroundings, partially recessed in the topography of the ground at below street level. The dark timber cladding plays with light and shadows so that the extension disappears in the shade of the forest.

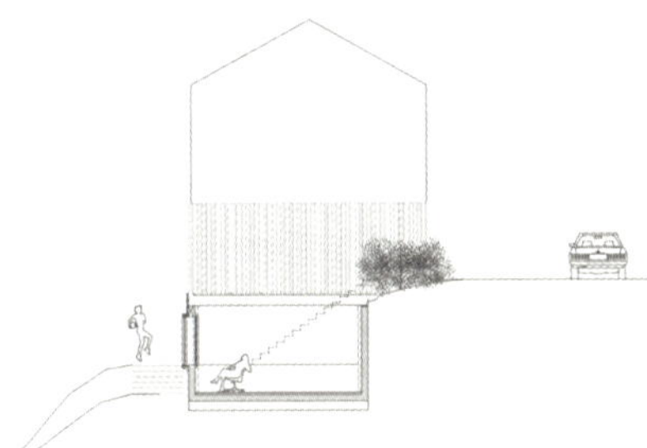

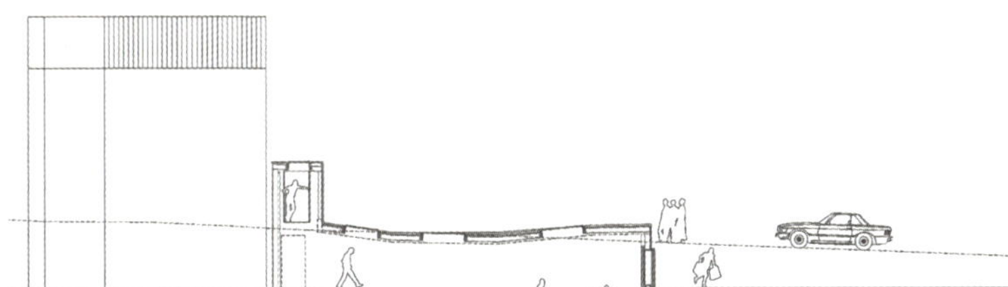

HALL 32

Never forget where you come from. A location bridging the gap between tradition and modernity.

Architects | Heinrich Böll Architekt BDA DWB
Location | Steinmüllerallee 10, 51643 Gummersbach, Germany
Completion | 1890 / 2013
Size | 2,680 sqm
Original use | brass foundry

For more than 125 years the Steinmüller company developed the central location and face of the city. In 2002 Gummersbach took over the grounds in the immediate vicinity of the downtown district in order to revitalize it. The revitalization concept of the grounds includes an extensive demolition of the manufacturing halls and the opening of a new access. Hall 32 will remain as a material witness of the building and production history of the location and will be fitted into the context of the other uses planned and the overall municipal development of the site. The hall will be used multi-functionally for events for 1,500 visitors, seminars for up to 400 participants and will feature a restaurant.

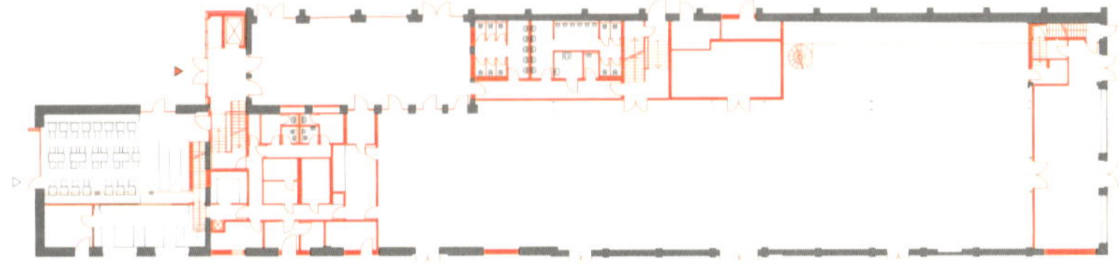

The approach of the design strives to retain the characteristic appearance and the historical legibility of the location. The basic structure and materiality of the façades have been kept for the most part in the conversion of the hall. The necessary additions are built as visible elements, leaving the heterogeneous appearance and legibility of the historical development.

FERRERIES 16

This is all about windows enabling this cube to be old and new at the same time.

Architects | CUBUS TALLER D'ARQUITECTURA
Location | Ferreries 16, Jafre (Alt Empordà), Girona, Spain
Completion | medieval times / 2010
Size | 142 sqm

The project, a rehabilitation of two houses in the old part of Jafre, investigates the reinterpretation of the traditional window form. This aim defines the building as part of a whole with the intention of joining the neighboring buildings in the block. On the other hand, through voids and strategies, double heights are created in the interior space. This adds depth to the views and brings in light from the outside. That in turn avoids an excessive trituration in a foreign style in favor of the character of the immediate surroundings.

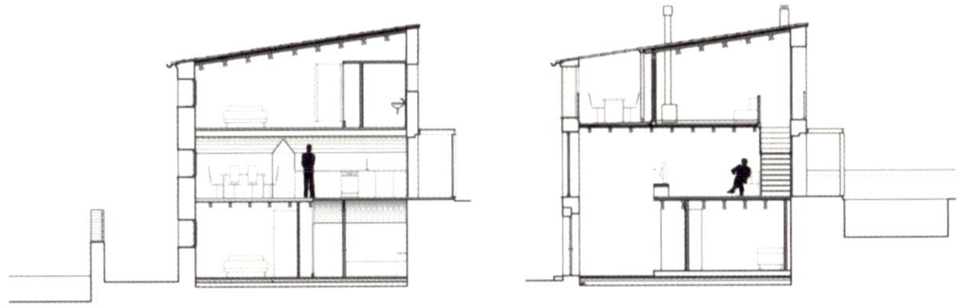

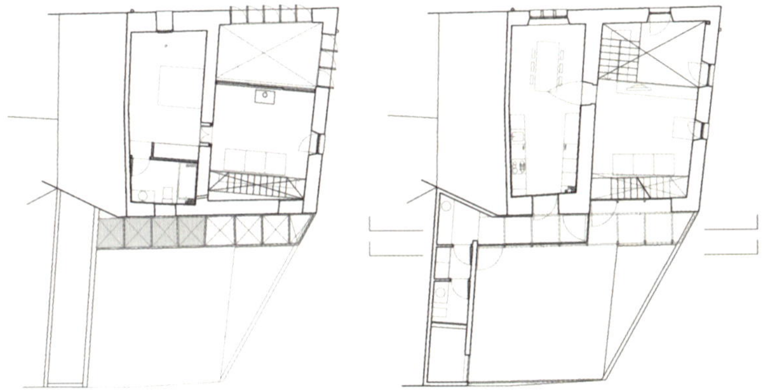

Architects | MaRGeN-Lab / IAAC
Location | Barcelona, Spain
Completion | 2011
Size | 144 sqm

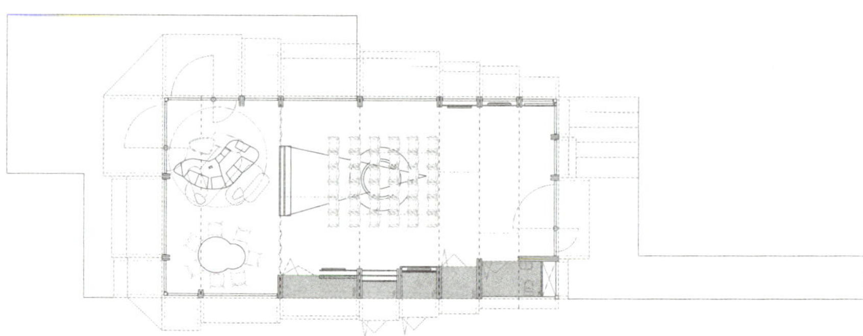

ENDESA PAVILION

Sheds a little light – this innovative pavilion is powered by the sun.

ENDESA pavilion is a self-sufficient solar prototype installed at the Marina Dock during the International BCN Smart City Congress. The pavilion is actually the prototype of a multi-scalar façade solar system. The façade is composed of modular components responsive to photovoltaic gaining, solar protection, insulation, ventilation and lighting. By means of a parametric design and digital fabrication a single component adjusts its geometry by responding with mathematical precision to the local environmental conditions. The ENDESA pavilion is an accessible device, technologically soft and easy to understand. Its geometry, construction, materials and energy and its climatic behavior are visible for the inhabitant. This transparency is essential to generate the needed environmental awareness.

Like a tree, the pavilion takes the energy from the surrounding energy flows. Each façade module produces electricity while controlling sun radiation, natural and artificial ventilation and natural and artificial light. Like a tree leaf, each façade component is generating energy and at the same time producing a protective microclimate. The pavilion is simply the result of the aggregation of these solar leaves qua façade components.

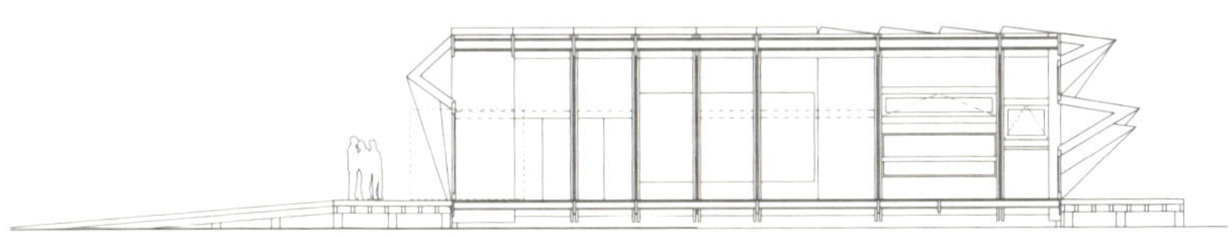

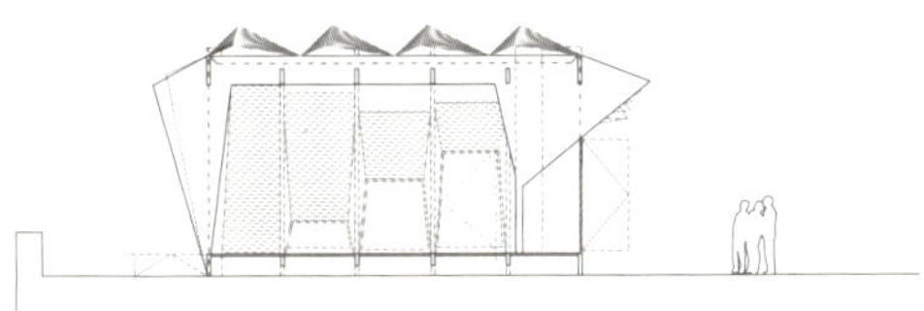

Villa CP is a restoration project which created a 21st century house inside an old stone structure. The existing stone walls have been largely rebuilt, with enormous openings towards the landscape linking the house to its spectacular surroundings: a National Park of cork oak with distant views towards the Mediterranean Sea. ZEST Architecture's work is always marked by sustainability, with materials and elements such as a natural pool whose water is filtered by plants and gravel, insulation with cork that is locally harvested and produced, clay and perforated panel finishes in the interior and heating and cooling through a geothermal installation.

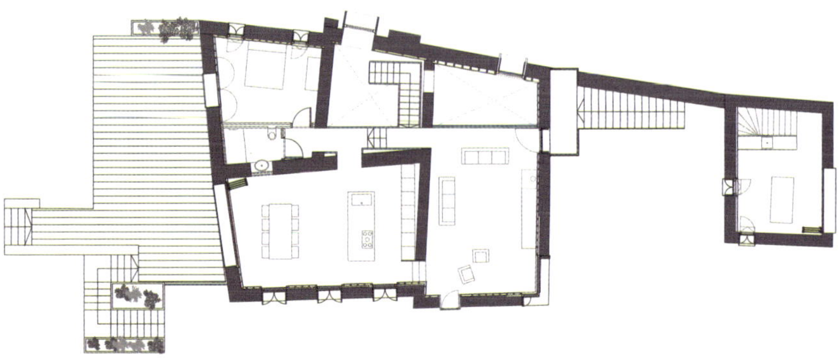

VILLA CP

At one with nature. The deluxe version of Mediterranean living.

Architects | ZEST Architecture
Location | Girona, Spain
Completion | ca. 1200 / 2013
Size | 440 sqm
Original use | farmhouse

The old and the new (which will age) strengthen each other in this project through their mutual tension. The old has been left visible with all its scars, while new materials such as Corten steel, wood and clay were chosen for the beauty of their natural imperfections and the way they become yet more beautiful in time. Rain, wind and the human touch will ensure a dignified and attractive age for this house over time.

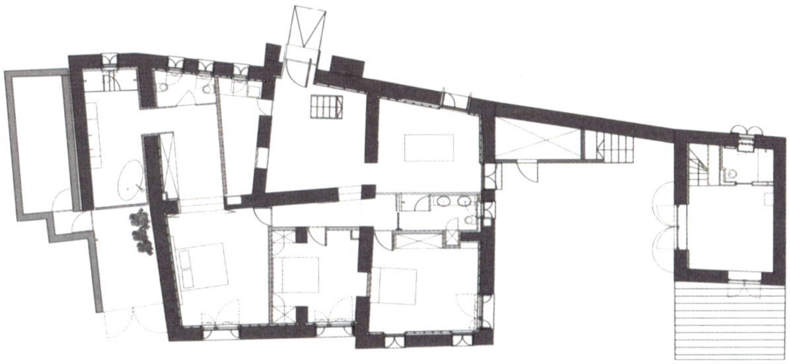

LONG MUSEUM WEST BUND

From coal to culture. A healthy dose of béton brut makes for a perfect home for an eclectic art collection.

Architects | Atelier Deshaus – Liu Yichun, Chen Yifeng
Location | No. 3398, Longteng Avenue, Xuhui District, Shanghai, China
Completion | 2014
Size | 33,007 sqm

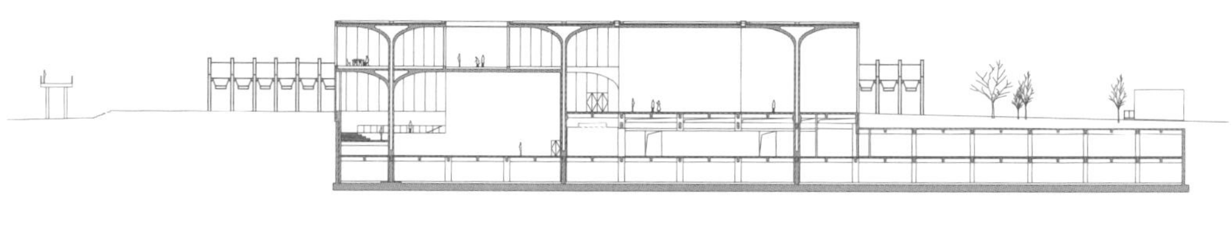

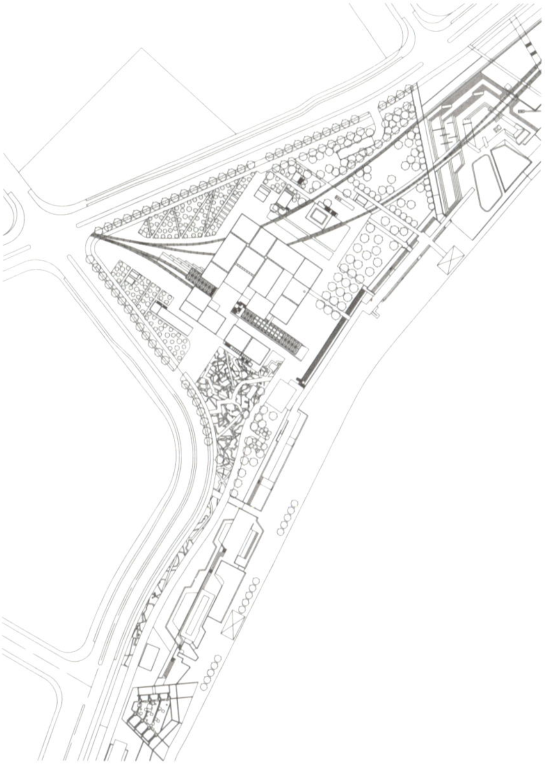

Long Museum West Bund is located at the bank of Huangpu River, Xuhui District, Shanghai Municipality. The site was used as the wharf for coal transportation. The new design adopts the cantilever structure featuring the 'vault-umbrella' with independent walls, while the shear walls with free layout are embedded in the original basement where they are connected with concrete with the original framework structure. The structure is also a visual echo of the Coal-Hopper-Unloading-Bridge at the wharf. The building's internal space has a kind of primordial and timeless charm while the rough cast finish of the concrete with the molding board seams and the bolt holes provide a back to earth sense as well.

The first underground floor of the original parking lot has been transformed into an exhibition space highlighted with multiple orientations because of the relative connection of the 'vault-umbrella' in different directions; in addition, the building technology has been integrated in the 'vault-umbrella' structure. For the space over the 'vault-umbrella', the walls and the ceiling are done in rough cast concrete, blurring their geometrical dividing lines.

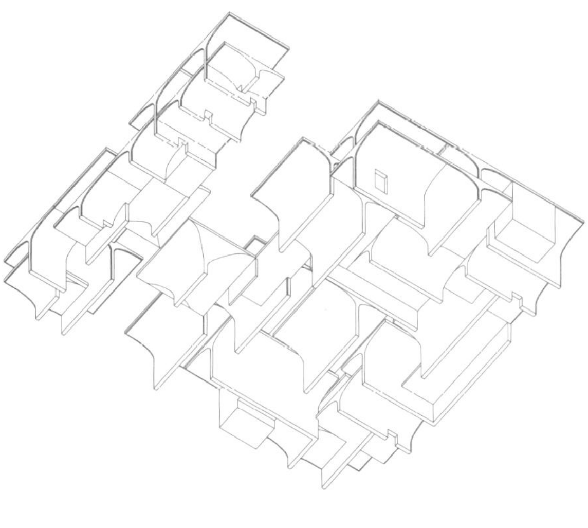

HAIDACHER'S KITCHEN

Is he researching new recipes? You will find out if the door is open.

Architects | Lukas Mayr Architekt
Location | 39030 Percha, Bolzano, Italy
Completion | ca. 1950 / 2013
Size | 40 sqm
Original use | workshop

Haidacher has been doing joinery work in South Tirol for 110 years. Until just a short while ago, the little workshop just stood there. Then Jochen Haidacher started thinking about converting the unassuming building into a studio for "Haidacher's Kitchen". The modest appearance of the hut is part of the idea. From the outside there are only vague hints that the building could house something special. Inside the gate another world opens up: what does a high-quality custom-made kitchen look like in the 21st century? How does one conceptualize a kitchen? What is the key to timeless design? All walls, including all building wall elements, the floor and the ceiling were rolled with black epoxy resin. These surroundings absorb the light while a huge kitchen occupies center stage.

Take another look: the studio is completely integrated in the surroundings. Visitors and potential customers drive to this location specifically. The black steel door shutters are only open when Jochen Haidacher is there.

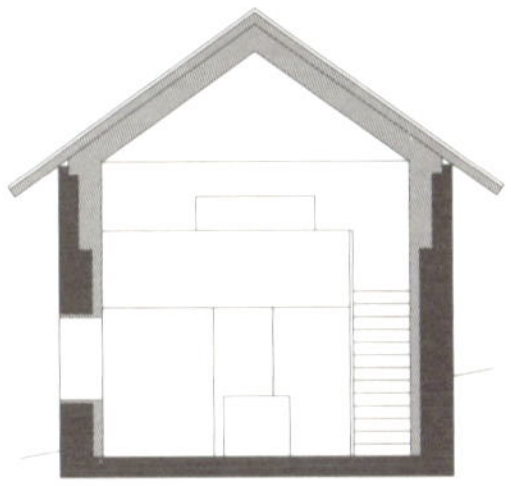

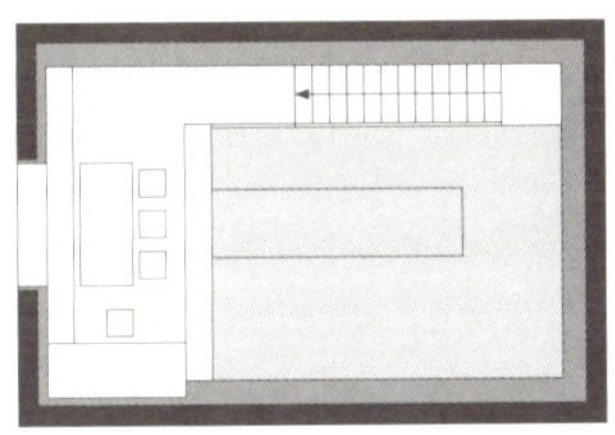

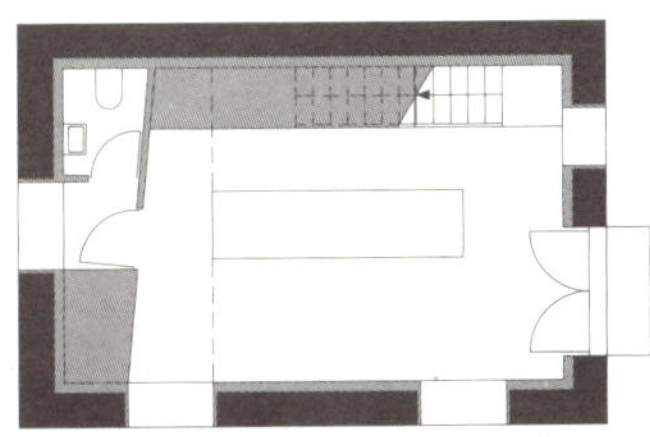

DOEHLER

Typical Brooklyn. Nowhere else can you find such a perfect mix of old and new, cozy and stylish.

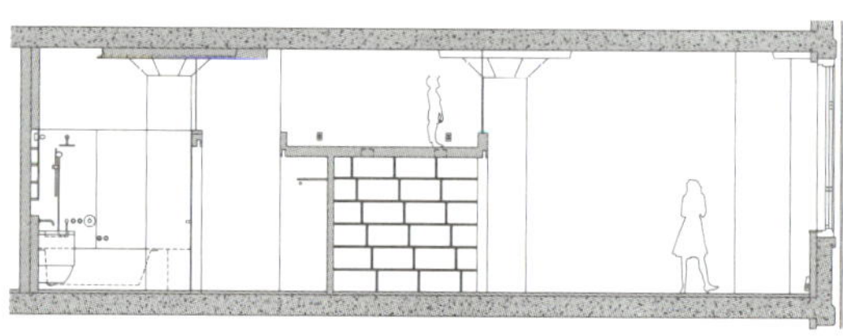

Architects | SABO project, Alex Delaunay
Location | Brooklyn, New York, USA
Completion | 1913 / 2014
Size | 124 sqm
Original use | industrial

Beneath the reclaimed ceiling, the new datum is defined by the height of a series of new partitions, custom-made cabinets, a walk-in closet, glass enclosures and a new mezzanine. The vertical contrast of opaque and transparent surfaces manages privacy while furnishing each space with natural light. The new connections between rooms establish a continuum that seems to expand each space beyond its limits. A built-in collection of wood containers stretches from the kitchen to the bedrooms, integrating stairs, display shelving, lighting and a home office. The bathroom was designed around a diamond shaped ceramic tile that determines all dimensions including the apartment's new datum. No less than three colors and nine shades are combined in bold graphic patterns and gradients that wrap seamlessly around the walls and floor, seemingly flooding the space.

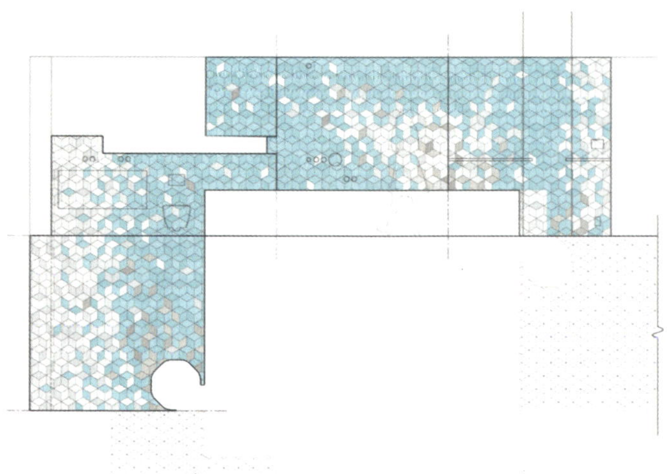

Doehler is the gut renovation of a Brooklyn loft located in a former die casting factory built in 1913. After a 1980s residential conversion, all concrete columns and ceilings were concealed. The removal of most partitions and a vast-dropped ceiling was the opportunity to restore the authenticity of the building as well as dramatically expand the space.

KEMENES VOLCANOPARK VISITOR CENTER

Fancy a dance on the volcano? Dark concrete walls and Corten steel invite you to enjoy the pure landscape.

Architects | Földes Architects
Project design team | Laszlo Földes, Csaba Balogh, Orsolya Tatar-Gonczi
Location | Celldömölk, Hungary
Completion | 2013
Size | 965 sqm

Upon entering the vast interior of the building, the visitor meets two engaging attractions. At first sight the vertically open space captures the eye. Five floors above, a small window lets in a beam of light offering the 'eruption' point on the flat roof. On the opposite side, the industrial materials of the façade appear consistent with the interior: naked concrete walls, dark gray resin flooring, steel staircase and corridor, and the Corten steel cubes also visible from the outside. The varied height and location of bridges link the different sizes and positions of the Corten boxes. These offer a range of functions, from screening rooms to interactive installations area, while presenting the fascinating history and typology of volcanoes.

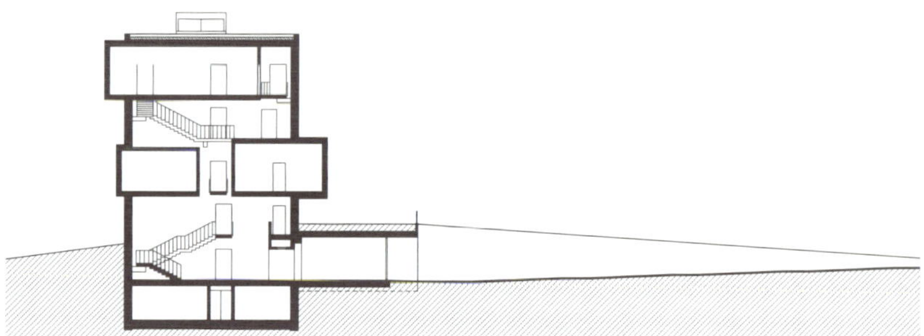

"Instead of literally translating the brief and creating a volcano shaped museum building, we wanted to capture the true identity of the location. According to our concept, the raw materials, the homogeneous gray of the concrete, the lava inspired color of the Corten steel, and the flue-like arrangement of the space, render the spirit and essence of a volcano." – Laszlo Földes, chief designer of Földes Architects.

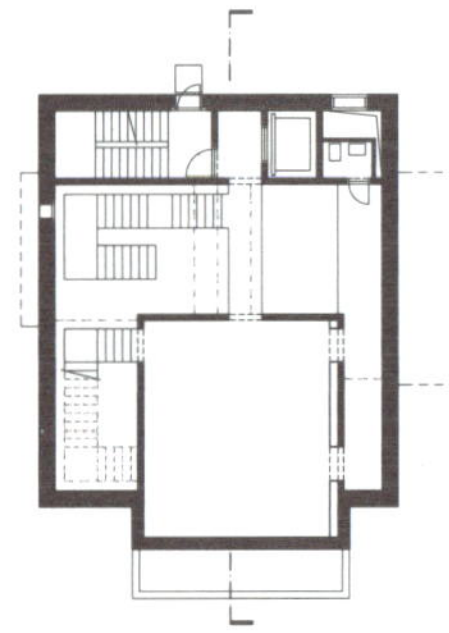

JD HOUSE

A space within a space. The perfect fusion of natural and man-made.

Architects | María Victoria Besonias, Luciano Kruk
Location | Mar Azul, department of Villa Gesell, Province of Buenos Aires, Argentina
Completion | 2009
Size | 149 sqm

Incorporating the maritime-forest microclimate, a low budget and a minimum maintenance requirement were the parameters for the esthetic-constructive system of the house. A particular feature was that in addition to the two bedrooms and their respective bathrooms, the social area had to be large enough to adapt to different uses as the users frequently have many guests. The solution was created by crossing two prisms perpendicularly and placing the structure in a forest clearing between the trees. The strong slope of the land was exploited to hide part of the building, reducing it to the presence of the built volume.

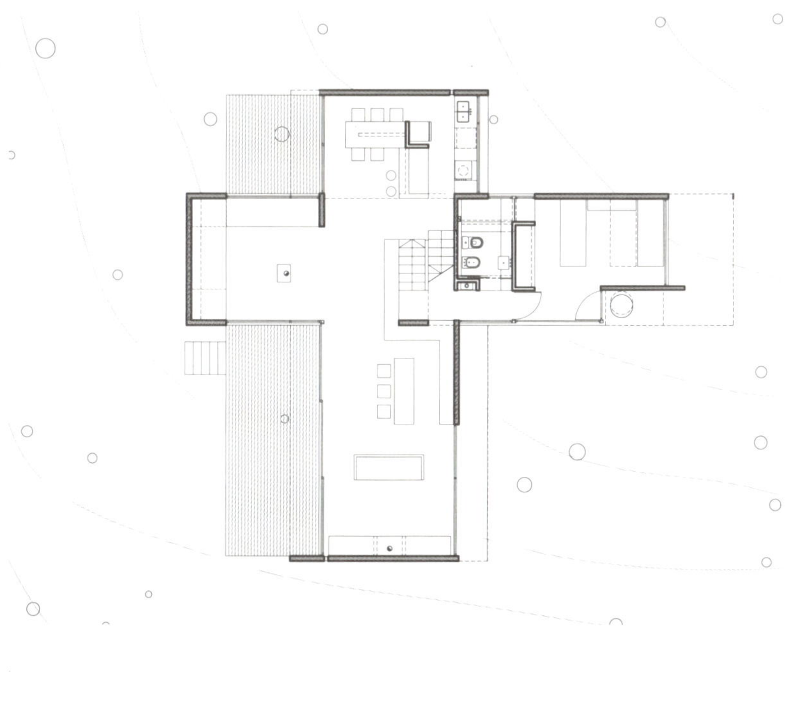

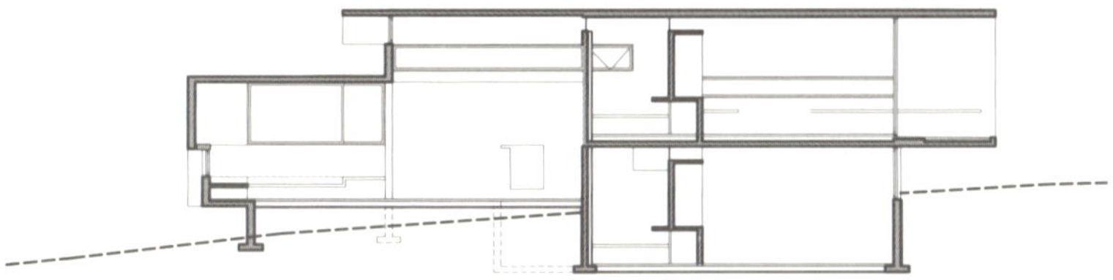

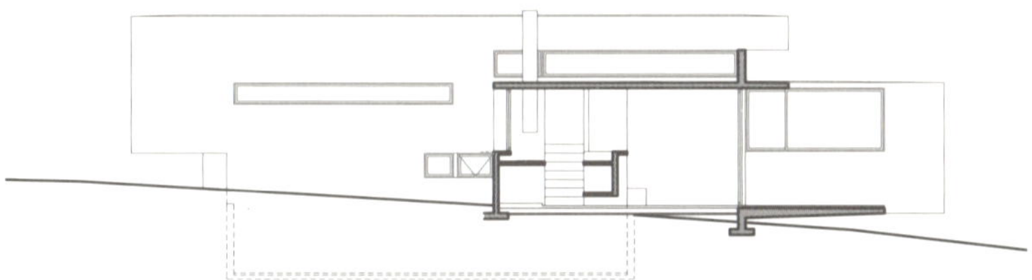

An outer skin made only of two materials — concrete and glass — resolves the integration with the landscape and the formal, structural and functional issues apart from the façades and the maintenance.

SÍTIO DA LEZÍRIA CONVERSION

Portuguese purism. Where once were horses, you'll now find flexible rooms in waxed cement and white painted wood.

The intervention site is located in Alcácer do Sal, Alentejo, a region truly strategic in Portugal because of its geographical, environmental and landscape features. The extensive areas for the production of salt due to the nearby Sado river provide strong economic development of the region, combined with the existing agricultural rich soil. Named "Sítio da Lezíria", the extensive property of approximately 14 hectares where the intervention takes place, is an ancient agricultural area with two existing buildings – the manor house, and the mews, rehabilitated by Atelier Data. The conversion of the mews into housing provided the opportunity to think about domestic space and also to test the way that people can re-inhabit ancient rural areas. This project is the result of the first phase of a broad strategy that aims to revive old agricultural land, combining new agricultural techniques with a new way of living.

Architects | Atelier Data
Location | Quinta da Lezíria, Alcácer do Sal, Portugal
Completion | 2012
Size | 210 sqm
Original use | stable

Keeping the original wooden structure of the roof and the circulation axis / central corridor (the horse path) and converting and redesigning the former stables into flexible housing units were the main design guidelines.

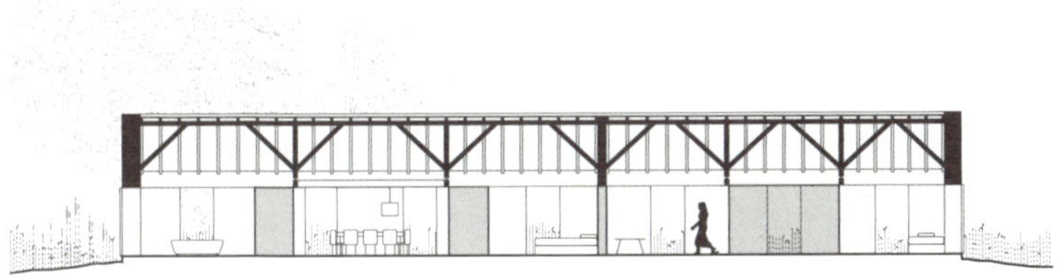

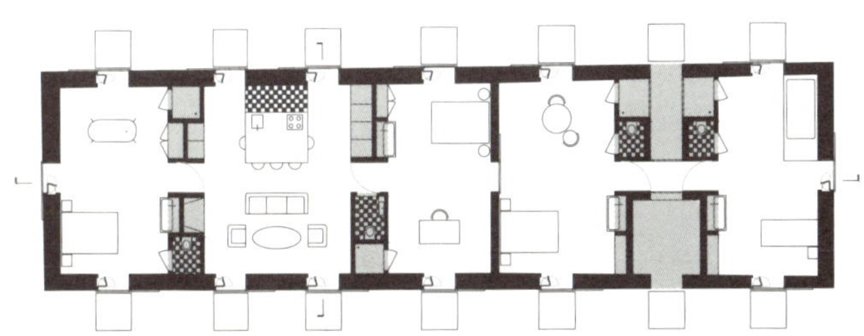

MODERN RUIN

Concrete, steel and sweat – that's what it takes to build great architecture!

Architects | Autotroph
Location | 3094 Agua Fria Street, Santa Fe, NM, USA
Completion | 2012
Size | 300 sqm

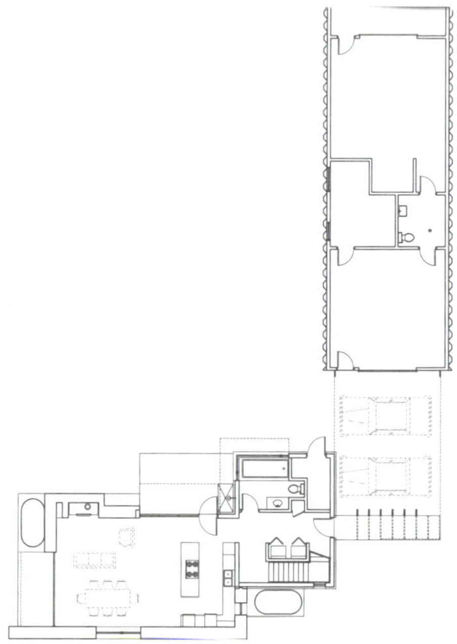

This home in the traditional historic community of Agua Fria Village, outside Santa Fe, New Mexico, exudes a rural industrial sensibility. A collaboration between architect and owner resulted in a selection of materials that imbue contemporary lines with a sense of ancient ruins. The open concept main room and kitchen are built with rammed earth while the two-story tower element is cast concrete with steel cladding. Much of the construction was done by the owner and many objects and materials were upcycled in the process. The architect used the tower element as a central pivot between the living space and the detached studio which presents a striking, monolithic view toward the street while creating an intimate and complex private space.

TOTAL

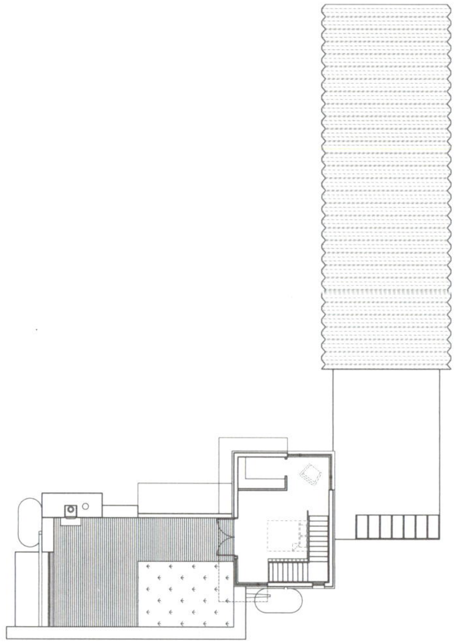

The juxtaposition of materials succeeds in instilling warmth and livability into a contemporary framework. While many contemporary buildings strike visitors as cold, this home's blend of thick, unplastered rammed earth and intentionally rough concrete creates a soulful sense of ease despite its rigorous lines. Generous fenestration allows light and landscaping to pour inside and invites the natural landscape to engage as an additional material component that anchors the building to a human scale.

LUKAS CHAPEL CONVERSION

Today the bathtub replaces the baptismal font. The resurrection of a sacral building which hasn't lost its spirit.

The task was to build two apartments in the former Chapel of St. Luke – an art-deco place of worship built in 1924 in a Bern city district. It had been completely disfigured in the 1970s. In order to keep the ground floor without supports and maintain the expansive church windows, the upper story apartment was suspended as a concrete box in the two-story former church space. The south façade, which had been originally closed, was opened up to the surrounding district and the garden with spacious sliding windows and cantilever balconies. Both apartments were equipped with minimum energy air-conditioning between the living rooms and bedrooms which provide fresh air via linear diffusers. Meals are now prepared and the delightful laughter of children resounds where once the pastor gave his sermon and the church organist gave played church hymns.

Architects | Morscher Architekten
Location | Balmweg 5, 3007 Bern, Switzerland
Completion | 1924 / 2014
Size | 715 sqm
Original use | chapel

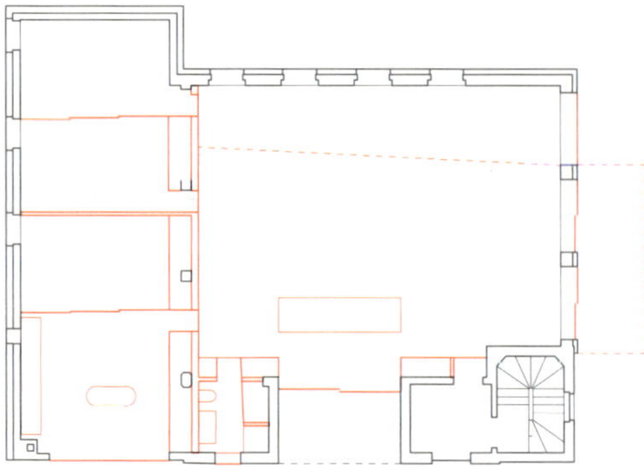

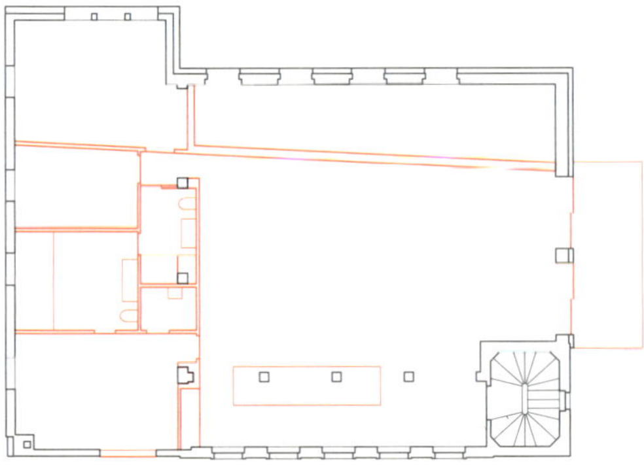

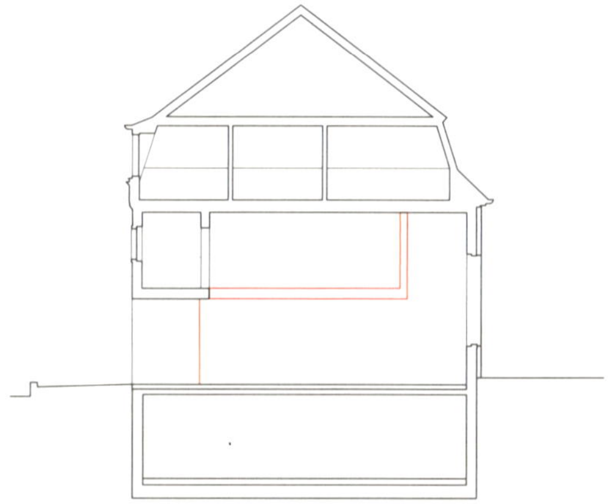

TANZWERK

The whole world is a stage. Fine arts in fine architecture.

Architects | spillmann echsle architekten ag
Location | 8005 Zurich, Switzerland
Completion | 2013
Size | 2,350 sqm
Original use | banana ripening facility of Migros supermarket

Tanzwerk is a dance school in the logistics department of the Migros supermarket chain in the industrial area of Zurich. Before the partial conversion project the spaces were used for ripening bananas and storage. Nine dance spaces, a large dance auditorium, an office area with work spaces as well as a variety of additional rooms were incorporated in the project. The extensive glazing system in combination with spatial divisions transports light deep within the building. A concrete spiral stair connects the spacious entrance hall with the lower levels. The materials which include concrete, glass and yellow chrome elements are minimalist and carefully selected.

13

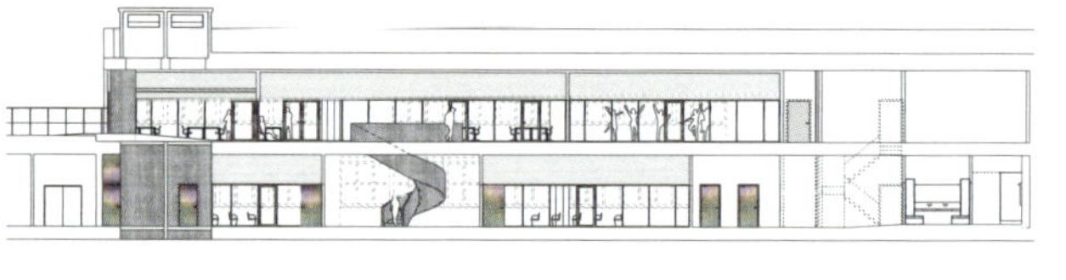

7
4

3-JÄHRIGER
VOLLZEIT-STUDIENGANG
START: 18. August 2014
4 7 8
WC
/Damen/Herren
Garderobe
Fluchtweg
freihalten!

BÍLKA BARN

Creating a win-win situation by using the Matryoshka-principle.

Architects | A2F ARCHITEKTEN
Location | 41501 Bílka, Czech Republic
Completion | 1886 / 2012
Size | 275 sqm
Original use | barn

The dilapidated barn was rebuilt as a residential building. The special challenge was to retain the decayed charm and along with it the attraction of the site. The conventional solution of the construction industry, with their insulation systems or new ersatz buildings did not apply here. The solution was a house-inside-a-house: within the massive walls set off by a surrounding footpath, is a new wooden structure offering modern living comfort. The new and the old form a symbiosis and assist each other in the structure and energy efficiency. And they produce a tension in the architectural space that contributes to the identity of the location.

The new building's appearance is marked by the wood used to construct it, thereby establishing a bridge to the existing barn: cracks and imperfections were deliberately retained, conveying the living character of the material. Parts of the supporting roof structure which had to be removed from the existing barn were used in the stairway. In order that the barn can be seen in the new space, a network of openings connects the inside with the intermediate space, as well as with the natural surroundings.

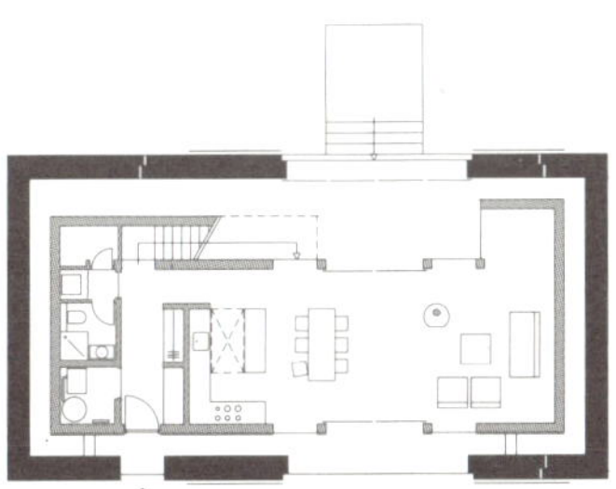

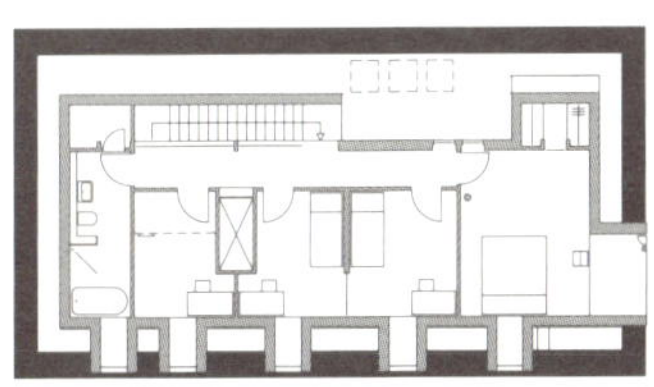

CASA BC

Enter infinite lightness and geometric forms. A house with an intimate relationship with its environment.

Architects | 3ARCH
Location | Bosque del Centenario 36, State of Mexico, Mexico
Completion | 2014
Size | 559 sqm

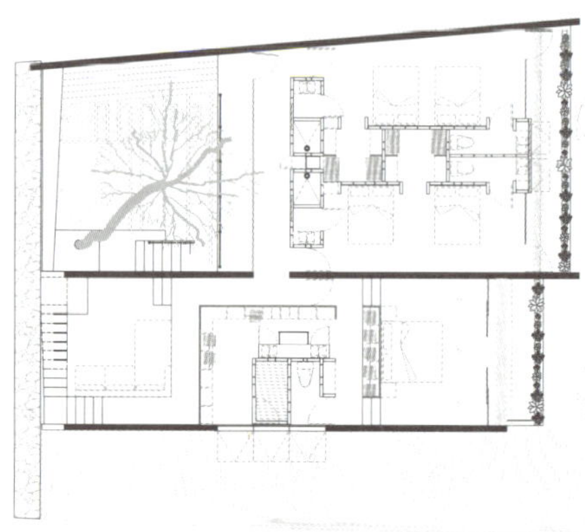

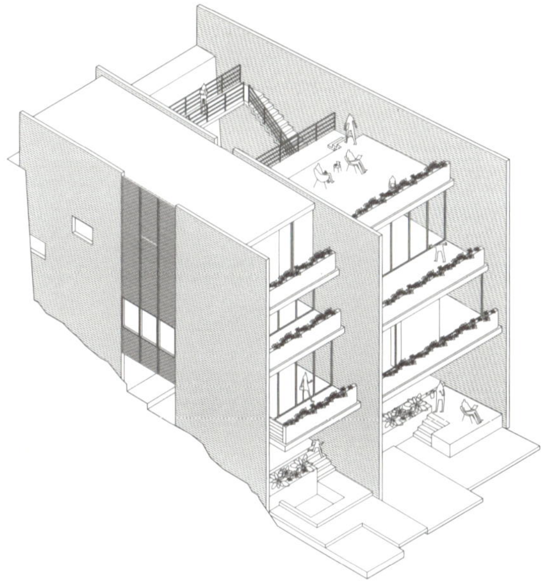

The house as a den. A place of isolation for reflection and rest, detached from the urban context and intertwined with the natural environment. The space outside never ends and the interior space never begins. Materials participate in the process of relation to the space outside; they adapt themselves, get older every day, change. The concrete walls isolate from the neighbors and frame the views; block boxes complement the spaces and services. The site is to be understood as a series of design responses: a cliff, a tree, a stone wall and canyon are the main components of the project.

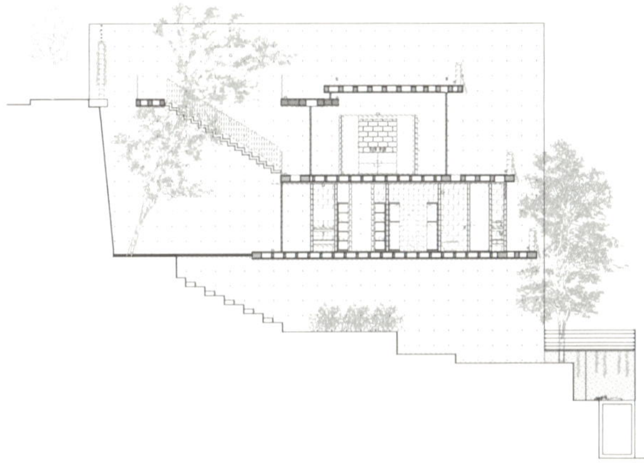

MARILIA PROJECT

For an impressive contrast of old and new, simply reuse the existing material and give it a supporting metal corset.

Architects | SuperLimão Studio
Location | São Paulo, Brazil
Completion | 1915 / 2014
Size | 450 sqm
Original use | residence

The history of this house, located a few meters from Paulista Avenue, starts at the beginning of 20th century according to the first blueprint dated 1915. Although modest in proportions compared to the big houses in the region, it is rich in details, having undergone several renovations over its almost one century of existence. The architects decided to maintain the house as a small survivor in a region today marked by high towers with glass façades. To adapt the smaller compartmentalized areas of the house to its new commercial purpose, the spaces were unified. These changes demanded large-scale structural interventions which the architects designed to show the contrast between the new and the old.

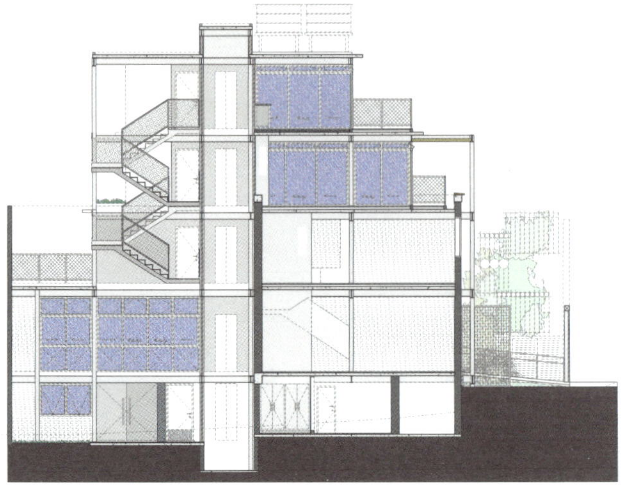

Due to the age of the house made of structural masonry, an independent steel structure was chosen as an exoskeleton to transfer the new loads directly to the new foundations, which were literally built under the existing house. In cases where the walls were compromised different restoration techniques were used, such as external beam connecting bolts which compress the walls and prevent them from collapsing like a house of cards.

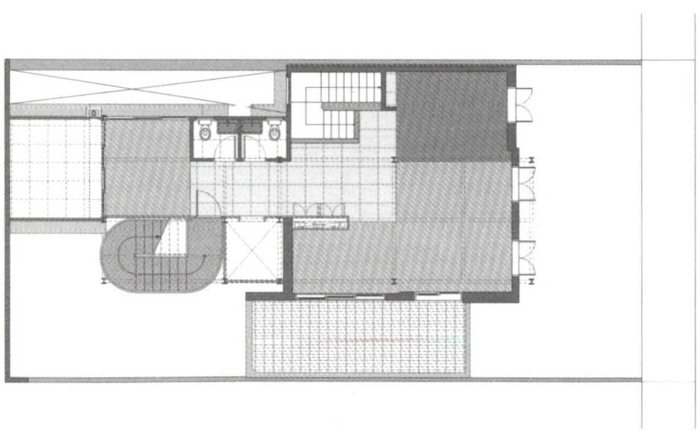

FUENSANTA HOUSE

Assemble your very own Greek-style temple – puzzle piece by puzzle piece.

Architects | MUKA ARQUITECTURA – Moisés Royo
Location | Ciudad Real, Spain
Completion | 2014
Size | 450 sqm

Muka Arquitectura's ribbed concrete residence completes the "first piece of the urban puzzle" for a largely undeveloped area of the Spanish city Ciudad Real. With plans for the adjacent plots uncertain, the architects designed a fortress-like block, featuring ribbed concrete walls topped by a pitched roof resting on two chunky abutments that project above the structure. A small doorway is recessed into the brown concrete façade. Three delicate glass boxes run the height of the façade, housing a bathroom, bar and staircase. White frosted glass, with a ridged texture that resonates with the concrete, veils the spaces while allowing light to penetrate the plan. A double-height void cuts through the core of the building. A narrow galley kitchen and adjoining dining room are set to one side of this space, with a toilet and storage room located directly below at basement level. A reception room, garage and utility room are located on the other level.

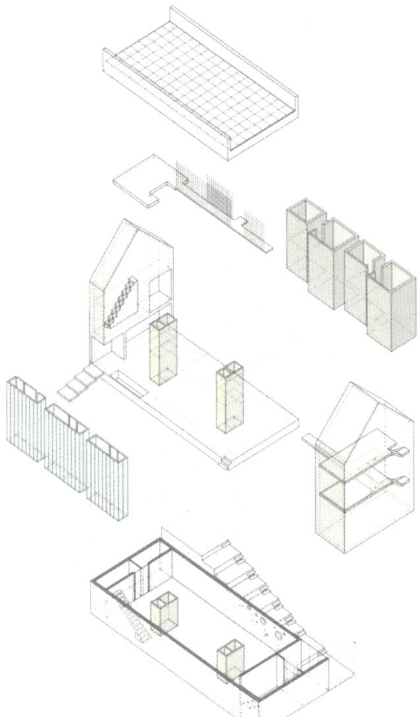

Porthole skylights are punched through the concrete ceiling and wall of the kitchen, throwing shafts of light onto the walls. Strips of light shine through slits in the steel base plate of the elevated walkway, which is attached to the ceiling by a row of metal cables. Sunlight entering the building through the three glass bays in the façade creates patterns on the textured concrete walls that line the space.

Nestled into a rural hillside, this unassuming structure serves as a studio for a musician to compose and reconnect with nature. With its exacting construction details and a restrained material palette, the building continues the tradition of Midwestern rural architecture and its proud legacy of esthetic sobriety and robust craftsmanship. A concrete plinth, carved into the hill, provides storage and supports a linear studio volume whose long sides are covered with a steel shroud. Glazed ends frame views into the landscape, providing access into the space and onto the green roof of the plinth. The steel shroud is slightly lifted off the plinth, teasingly exposing a narrow clerestory that allows the studio to 'float' above its base. At night, a soft glow emanates from the clerestory into the dark countryside.

Architects | Johnsen Schmaling Architects
Location | Spring Prairie, Wisconsin, USA
Completion | 2012
Size | 35 sqm

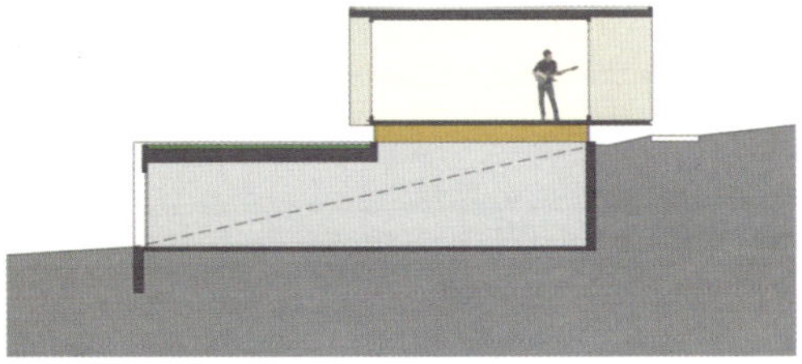

STUDIO FOR A COMPOSER

Country music in the countryside with nature as its audience – architecture in its purest form.

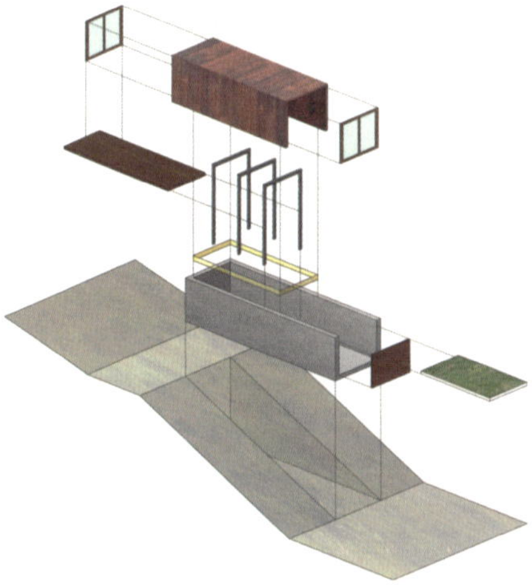

The carefully detailed steel envelope turns the building skin into an ever-changing canvas, its warm color of rust echoing the hues of the derelict farm equipment left behind in the area's abandoned fields, which along with the oil slicks and roller marks from the steel mill leave their individual traces to the mercy of the elements, juxtaposing the building's formal restraint with a quixotically unpredictable veneer.

DAOÍZ Y VELARDE CULTURAL CENTER

No claustrophobia here: space, space and more space!

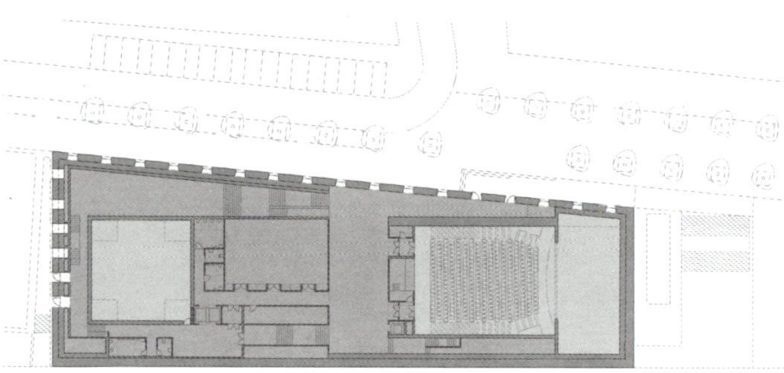

The idea was to respect the basic geometry of the existing building, as well as its saw-tooth metal structure and the brick-built façade. The interior space has been emptied to create a container for the cultural center, which is divided into two areas with separate entry points and circulation areas, retaining a strong visual and spatial connection between them while keeping open the possibility of adapting them to different types of events. A newly created intermediate space separates the former container from the new uses to bring the character of the existing building to the fore and set up a protective filter with the exterior. These intervening spaces establish visual connections that foster variations in the spatial experience. A generous communal space has been created at the entry points; it is a place for meeting, information and exhibitions, which works as a covered agora, as if the square outside extended into the building.

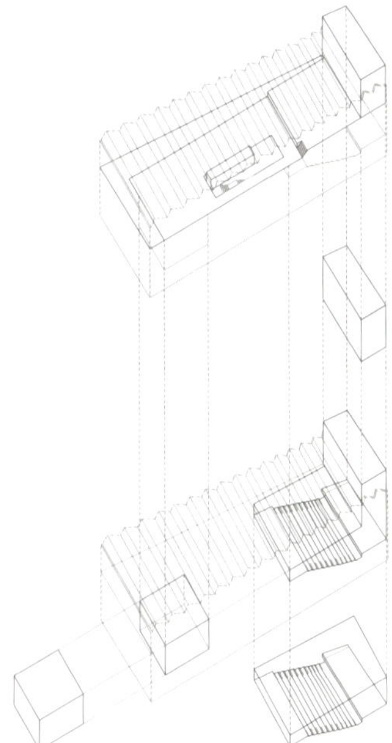

Architects | Rafael De La-Hoz
Location | Calle Alberche, Venturada, Madrid, Spain
Completion | 2013
Size | 6,850 sqm
Original use | industrial and military construction

The most striking aspect of this project may be the new volume of the stage box which reaches out of the roof and announces that the function of this refurbished and highlighted building is quite different from the original.

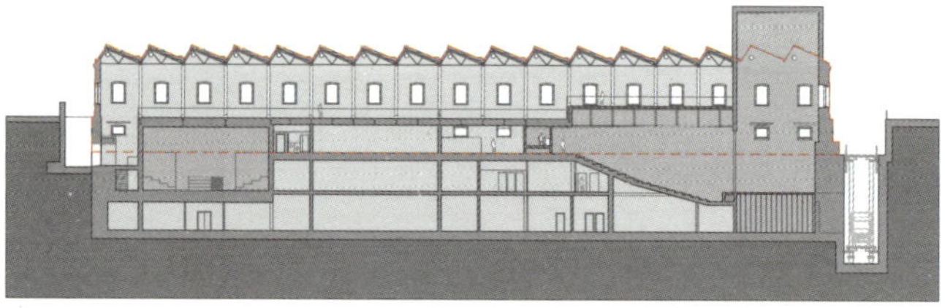

A O Í Z

V E L A R

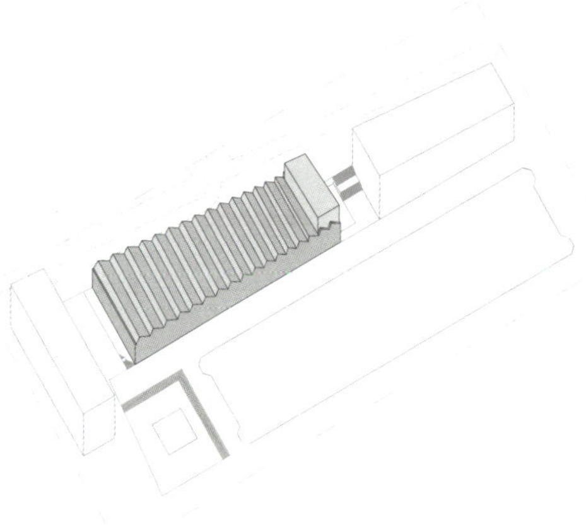

PALAZZO DI VIGONOVO "CAMPIELLO"

If you want to know something about the history of Campiello, just read the façade.

3ndy Studio was contracted for the renovation of the Campiello, which was inaugurated in September 2011. The project achieved its goal of renovating a very important part of Vigonovo by realizing a new meeting place in the historical center. Reviving such a place and restoring its ancient glory means recalling the voices that lived in it, putting together the historical fragments, the pieces of daily life and tradition that can be found and traced out on a sheet of paper. This huge piece of paper has become, in the project of the Campiello, a mammoth sculpture made of 190 sheets of Corten steel spread out over 300 square meters which are to be read as the enigmatic page of a book. The idea is to reestablish the design of the nineteenth-century building, destroyed by a fire.

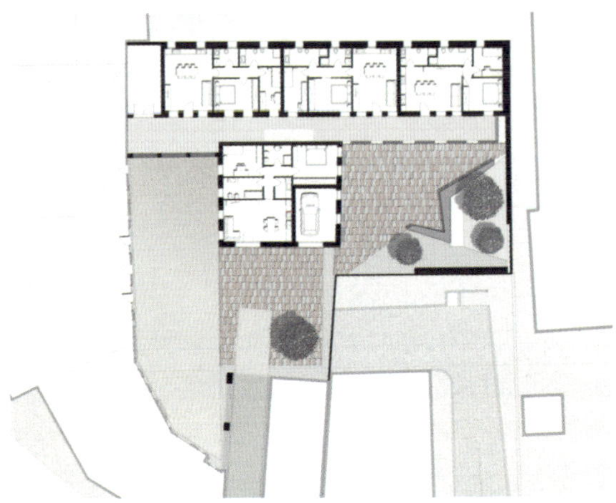

Architects | 3NDY STUDIO
Location | Via Veneto 5d, Vigonovo, Venice, Italy
Completion | Napoleonic age / 2011
Size | 300 sqm
Original use | horse stable

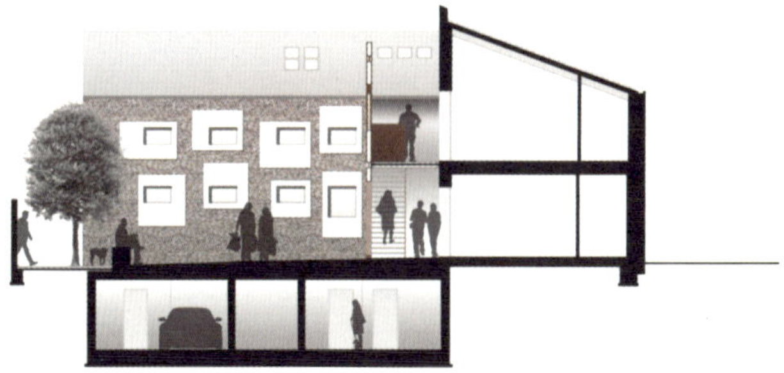

The façade designed by 3ndy Studio reproduces the dimension of the destroyed one, while suggesting the moment of time on the plaster. In order to complete the exclusive façade, 3ndy Studio involved Philippe Daverio, art critic, and Giorgio Milani, a sculptor from Piacenza, to take part in the large scale artistic operation. By carving the words and the spaces between them in the panels of Corten steel Daverio and Milani enriched the sculptural page.

HOUSE IN NISHIOCHIAI

So much more than just stairs! Living the Heraclitian thought of "panta rhei" - everything flows.

Architects | SUPPOSE DESIGN OFFICE
Location | Nishiochiai, Shinjuku, Tokyo, Japan
Completion | 2013
Size | 96 sqm

The owner wishes to enjoy a house with beautiful light and rich spatial meanings. The architects proposed a new style of the Japanese small residence in the context of the big city. Usually, stairs and corridor spaces are seen as auxiliary space. In this house the stairs extend into the rooms creating a blurry space without defined borders. This auxiliary space becomes integral to the design which the owners can designate with meaning as they choose. The spiral room and the large atrium void create a stack effect for natural ventilation. Openings and canopies are placed sparingly to create just enough light into the space, resulting in a cozy interior with a dramatic tranquility.

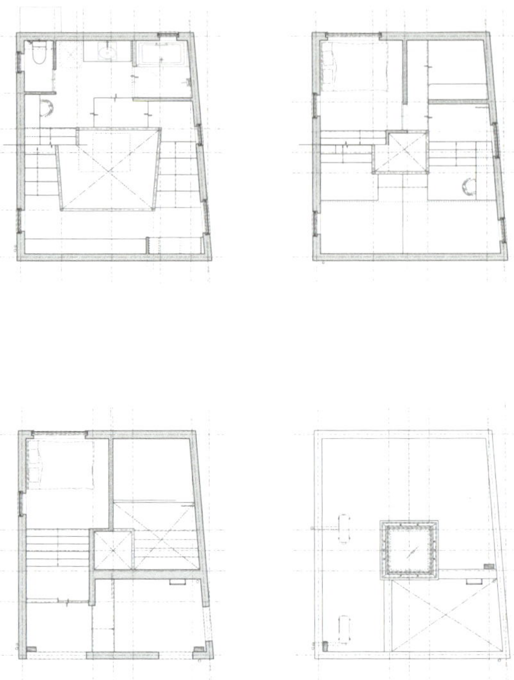

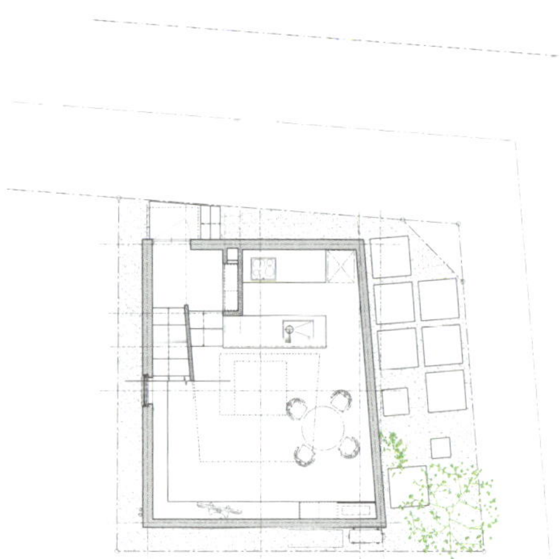

Architects | Westphal Architects
Location | Konsul-Smidt-Straße 20–26, 28217 Bremen, Germany
Completion | 1959 / 2013
Size | 30,102 sqm
Original use | warehouse, cargo handling shed

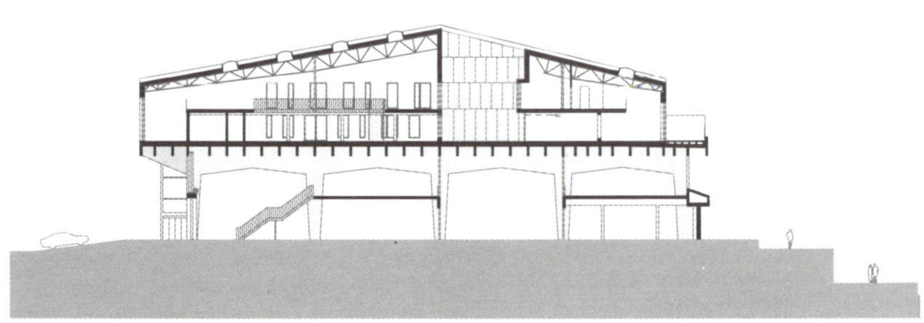

SCHUPPEN EINS

From rags to riches, from fruit to cars. The perfect showcase for vintage cars.

The port of Bremen with the old harbor district to the right of the Weser is increasingly developing into a vibrant city district. With its striking architecture, the Schuppen Eins, located directly in the Europahafen, plays a prominent role in the further development of the port city. This harbor related cultural monument was erected in 1959 as a two-story general cargo handling shed with a length of 400 meters. While retaining its original industrial architecture, it has adapted to the changing times and now hosts a technology and adventure center for historical automobiles, with apartments and office space. The nine-meter-high ground floor is set off by a boulevard passing through it and a spacious entryway. Oldtimers are on display, restored, maintained, stored and sold here. Loft sized offices and apartments are located in the upper floor of the shed. Users can ascend with their automobiles via a roomy auto lift directly onto the upper floor.

The architects were constantly preoccupied up until the final submission with retaining the large-scale and decayed charm of this historical building after the conversion, while finding a design solution for a 50-meter-wide building.

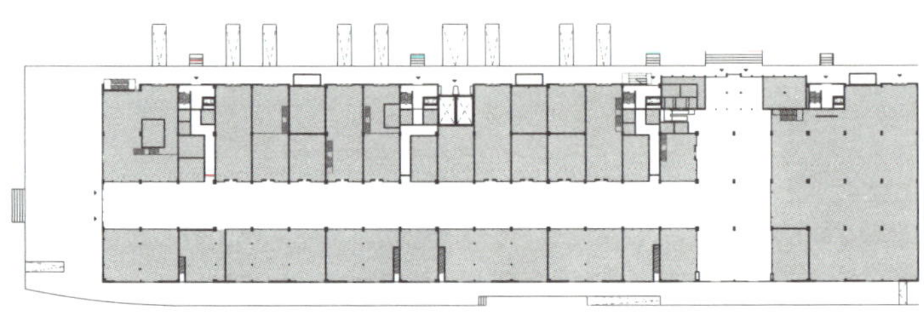

team neusta

Architects | Förstberg arkitektur och formgivning
Location | Linköping, Sweden
Completion | 2015
Size | 135 sqm

HOUSE FOR MOTHER

Cool yet warm, functional yet comfortable – And all that times two! Mamma mia!

The house is divided into two parallel volumes slightly offset from each other, thus creating spaces both in front of and behind the building. Oriented to the park in the north and the alley in the south, the two adjacent gables emphasize the overall theme for the area: narrow plots and a variation of housing types. The first volume contains the kitchen, dining room and living room, with the bathroom and laundry room housed in a smaller cabin within the structure. The second volume, partly in two levels with a less inclined roof, houses the bedrooms and a small studio.

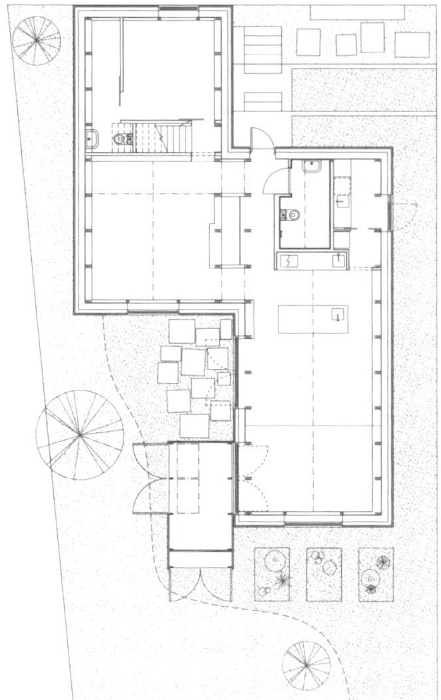

Façades and roof are covered with raw, corrugated aluminum while the interior is warm with an exposed timber structure and walls lined with plywood. The polished concrete floor folds up along the perimeter of the building and turns into a bench and shelf.

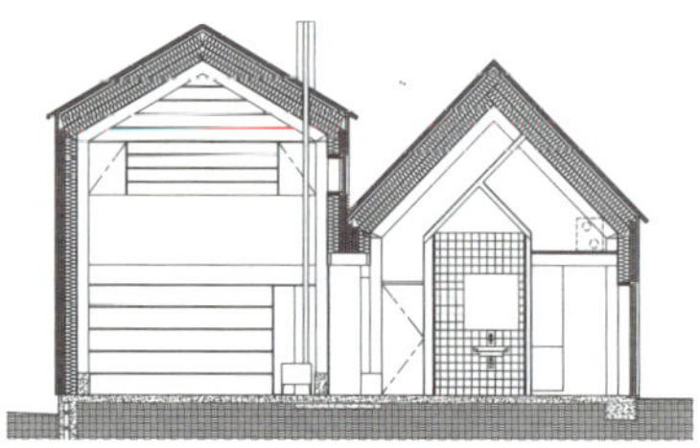

HOUSE OF VANS LONDON

Why choose between skateboarding, having a drink or seeing a movie if you can have it all at the same time at the same place?

Architects | Tim Greatrex and Hellicar&Lewis
Location | Arches 228–232 Station Approach Road, London, UK
Completion | 2014
Size | ca. 2,500 sqm
Original use | Waterloo tunnel station

The House of Vans London is a new mixed-use creative venue for Vans enthusiasts and those interested in skateboarding culture. It has been established as a place to participate in the cultural lineage of skateboarding that has defined the Vans brand since 1966, combining skateboarding, art, film and music. The new venue includes an art gallery, "Vans labs" creative spaces, a screening room, live music for 850 people, a premium café, numerous bars and a three-tier indoor concrete skate park. The House of Vans London sits within the 150 year old brick arches of the railway lines heading out of Waterloo station next to London's famous graffiti street, Leake Street. The site was previously used by the Old Vic Theatre. The area of the site is approximately 2,500 square meters and contains five separate long tunnel spaces.

HOUSE OF
LDN VANS

The five separate tunnels of the site are unified with the large and impressive rubber floor. The iconic sole of the Vans shoe inspired the layout of the hexagon and diamond pattern, with the strip of hexagons of the sole made to align with an enfilade of arches to define a main axis and corridor through the venue.

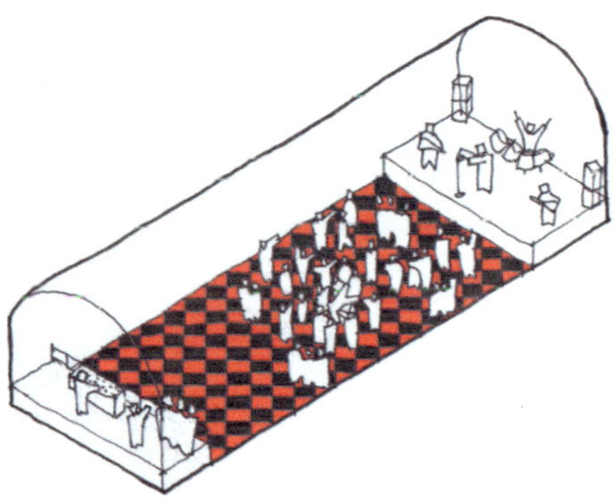

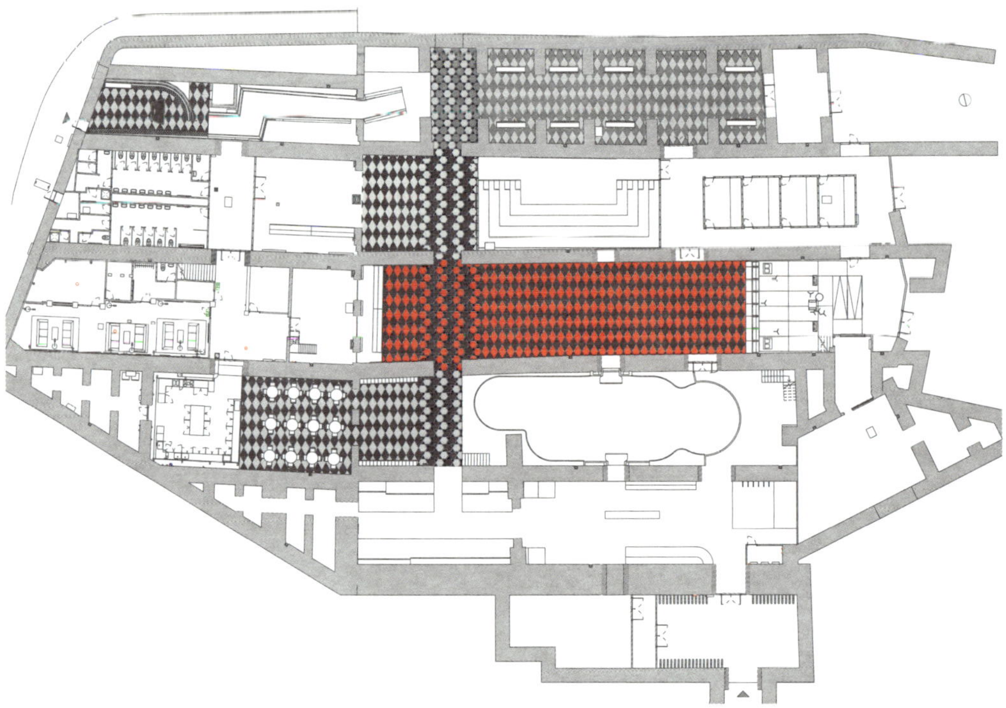

THE
WALL
SE1
EGGS
TWO HANDS
ONE HAND
MORE
COUNTER MENU

HOUSE OF
VANS

FOREST RETREAT

Balance is everything! Spiritually, physically and statically.

Architects | Uhlík Architects – Petr Uhlík, Jan Šorm, Přemysl Jurák
Location | Central Bohemia, Czech Republic
Completion | 2013
Size | 16 sqm

The enclosed black object made of charred wood contains an interconnected space measuring 3.1 x 5.8 meters. In the entryway there is a platform with headroom for a standing person; this part is accessed by a large glassed-in surface revealing a view. The remaining part of the object rises gradually towards another opening facing the tree crowns. There is also a special location for resting. Each step can be used as a sleeping place. Underneath the stairs there is storage space; turning one of the benches over creates another double bed. The space is suitable for dwelling, smaller events, performances or just meditation. Both glassed-in openings can be closed by shutters, the larger one with a pulley and a hand winch.

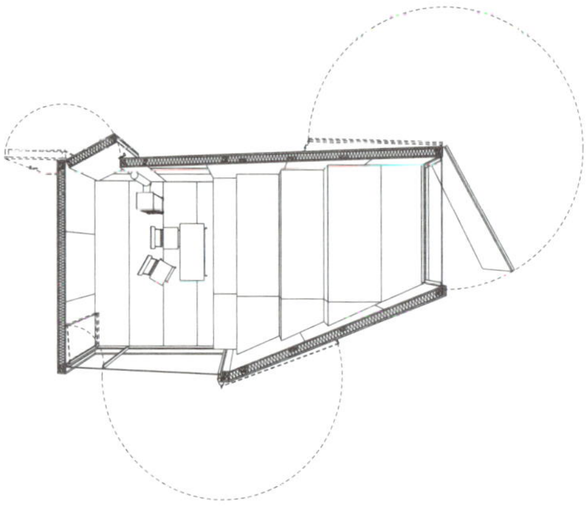

The object offers a hideaway in the countryside. It is located in an area between Central and South Bohemia where the client comes from and which he has loved visiting since his childhood. He took the architects to a forgotten spot in the midst of fields, woods and meadows, full of boulders. The building material was on hand: lumber came from a nearby forest while local sources and craftsmen were drawn on for labor and the rest.

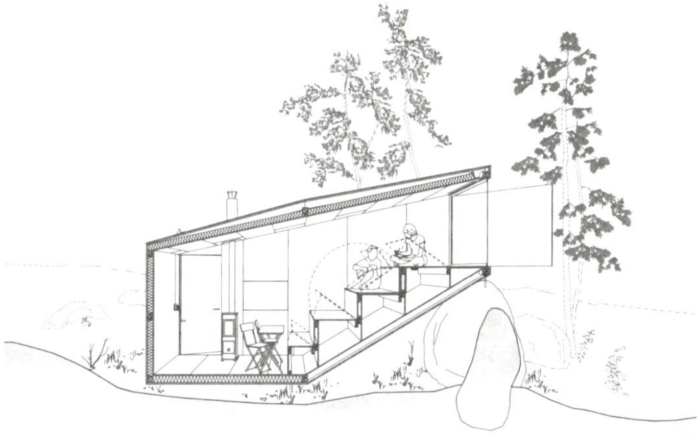

The core space of the gallery, the main exhibition hall, is lifted up in a black steel box in the center of the old building, under a special double-roof skylight, which illuminates the exhibition space with gently diffused top-light. The enclosed exhibition box connects to the ground floor via two partially glazed halls. On the one hand several free-standing functional blocks support the elevated main hall, while on the other hand defining the ground floor space and functions that contain a showroom, an auditorium, an art shop and related dividable multifunctional spaces. The ground floor is open in all directions to the original factory grounds, as well as to the surrounding natural landscape.

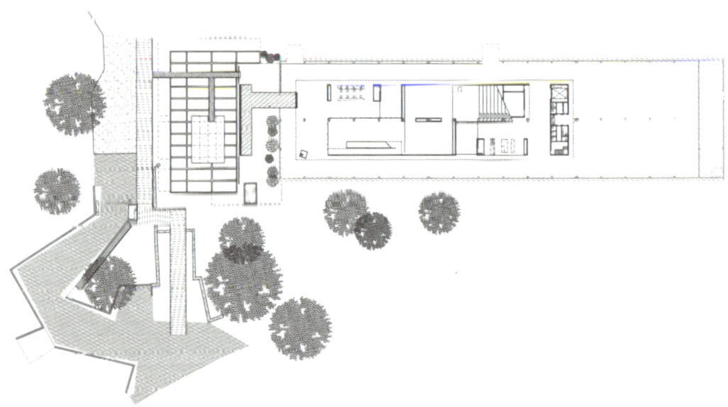

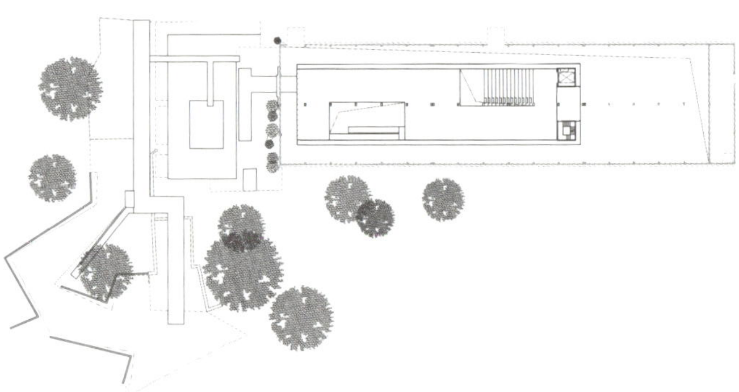

MJH ART GALLERY

Thinking outside the box made easy and very fashionable.

Architects | O-office Architects
Location | Kuipeng Road, Shenzhen, China
Completion | 1989 / 2014
Size | 3,740 sqm
Origina use | packing workshop of Honghua Dyeing Factory

A sequence of landscaping walls, pedestrian and vehicle ramps derived from the topography were designed to link the gallery's main entrance to the lower plaza that connects the suburban road. This landscape path from the plaza to the gallery detours between nature and artefacts, industrial and post industrial landscape, creating an experience of the whole time line of the site's history.

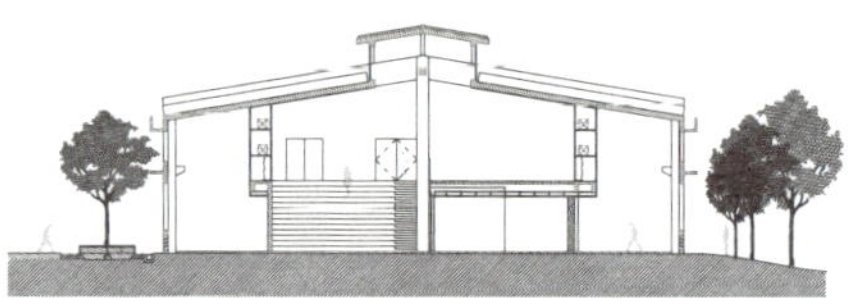

HABITAT DA NUS

Living history. A successful reinterpretation of traditions.

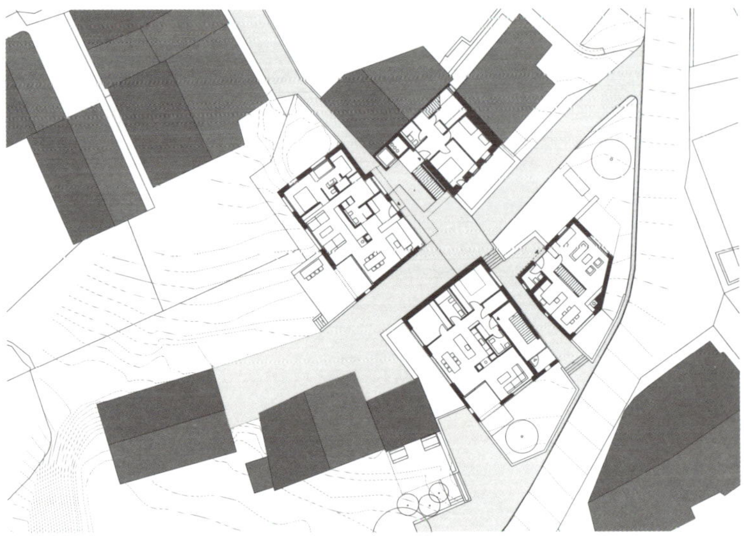

Architects | K&L Architekten
Location | 7017 Flims, Switzerland
Completion | 1757 / 2011
Size | 870 sqm
Original use | farmhouse with two barns

New life and living in the old village. In the middle of Flims a diverse apartment project was created: a smaller new building, two replacement buildings for reconstructed barns and the conversion of an existing historical property opened up possibilities for a multitude of independent, unconventional and sophisticated apartments, including residential as well as vacation dwellings. The architects investigated both the relationships of volumes to each other in the developed village conglomerate and the interpretation of modern forms of living in the historical context. Every apartment has its own private outdoor space, gallery levels offset the limited room heights in the existing structure, and exciting floor plan solutions with different openings generate completely individualized apartments.

The structured thermo-concrete façade with the board shuttering and the delicate projections and recesses recalls the tectonics of the old barns and reinterprets the traditional construction with a wood construction on top of a massive plinth.

10 SMART SQM

Smart homes for clever heads.

Architects | Tengbom Architects
Location | Virserum, Sweden
Completion | 2013
Size | 10 sqm

To successfully build affordable student housing requires innovative thinking and new solutions. The area in each unit has been reduced from the current requirement of 25 square meters to 10 square meters by legal consent. This truly compact-living flat still offers a comfortable sleeping-loft, kitchen, bathroom and a small garden with a patio. Through an efficient layout and the use of cross laminated wood as a construction material the ecological impact and carbon footprints have also been significantly reduced. Energy efficiency is a key issue when designing new buildings. Choosing the right material and manufacturing methods is vital to minimize the carbon emission. Therefore wood was chosen for its carbon positive qualities, which as a renewable resource can be sourced locally to minimize transportation. The method of manufacture was chosen because of its flexible assembling technique which can be done on site to reduce construction time.

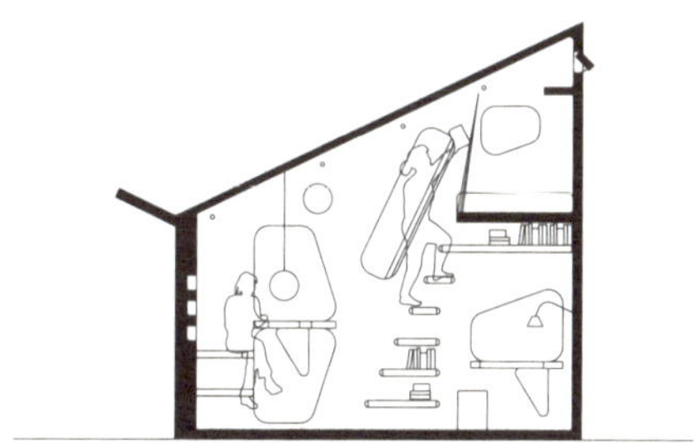

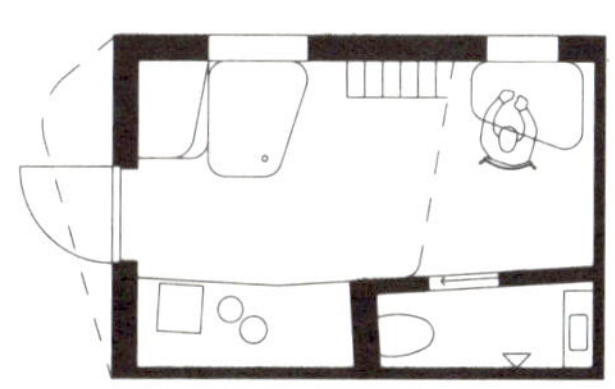

Gorki Apartments is located in Berlin's vibrant hub near Rosenthaler Platz. Off the beaten track from the ordinary hotel environment in Berlin's trendy Mitte district, Gorki Apartments offers 34 individually designed apartments as well as two luxury penthouses with unsurpassed levels of style and comfort in an exclusive "Gründerzeit" (Wilhelminian style) ambience. The distinctive and luxurious apartment interiors were styled by the Franco-German architect and interior designer Sandra Pauquet in collaboration with architect Kim Wang. Classic design pieces by Eiermann, Dixon, Hansen, or Knoll mixed with vintage finds from the local flea markets and contemporary items represent the generic spirit found in Gorki Apartments.

GORKI APARTMENTS

Berlin's rough charm and Russian extravagance make a fascinating couple!

Interior designer and architect | Sandra Pauquet in collaboration with Kim Wang architect
Location | Weinbergsweg 25, 10119 Berlin, Germany
Completion | early 20th century / 2014
Original use | housing

To support the apartment building ambience the designers replaced all room numbers in the building with fictitious names. In addition, every apartment received its very own doorbell and mailbox.

1
Etage

DARPER'S BASTION CONVERSION

Welcome to Transylvania. Explore its medieval history from the inner Corten steel tower.

Brasov is one of the Transylvanian cities built in the Middle Ages by German colonists. Most of its fortifications were demolished in the 19th and 20th centuries. The Darper's Bastion is part of this fortification system. Having been abandoned, fragile elements, like sentinel walks and staircases, vanished completely, leaving just the circular wall. During excavations remains of older walls were found. The architects proposed to locate the information center in an independently standing interior tower that does not affect the structure or the exterior image of the bastion. The new tower (158 square meters) starts in the basement with a minimal footprint. It enhances the perception of the bastion at its full height and accesses the rebuilt sentinel walks.

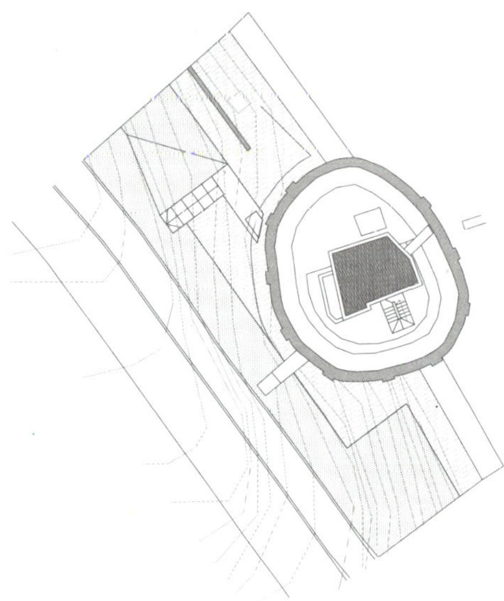

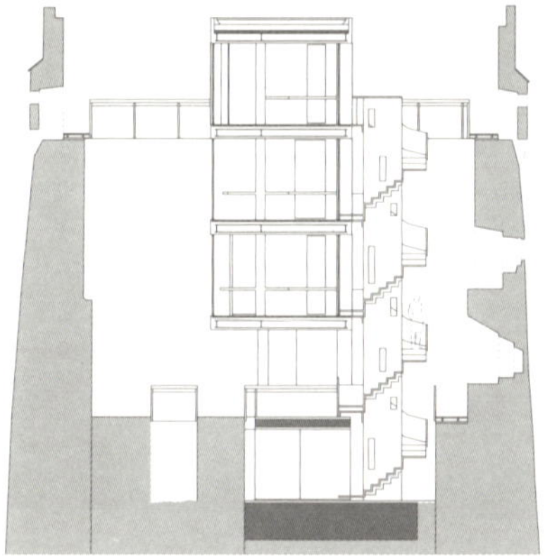

Architects | POINT 4 SPACE
Location | Brasov, Romania
Completion | 1450–1455 / 2011
Size | 158 sqm
Original use | Darper's Bastion

Except for the concrete foundation, the whole structure can be dismantled and reused, allowing future interventions into the bastion. In addition to closing the building, the 75 x 300 cm Corten steel panels also brace the metal frame. The project acknowledges the fact that the bastion was planned, built and used for combat. The visual, audio and physical experience reveals the original tension. The new tower becomes a mechanism for exploration, a new interior-exterior space layer.

GUSSWERK EXTENSION

The bell foundry's new clothes. Salzburg shows up for creative industries.

Architects | ARGE Erweiterung Gusswerk
hobby.a / LP architektur / CS-architektur / Strobl Architekten
Location | Söllheimerstraße 16, Salzburg, Austria
Completion | 2012
Size | 13,168 sqm

In the course of a moderated competition with the four architecture firms for the first foundry expansion in 2005, the location is expanding again. New spaces for the retail and hotel trades and for administrative uses are being created on about 16,000 square meters. The extension includes the development of the north-east section on Söllheimerstraße and a structural and spatial connection to the existing quarter via the center at the foundry tower. The new structure incorporates existing dimensions and spatial principles and completes the section with a plinth floor on the north-east side. The physical extension of the building, and the development as a communicative element in the urban fabric are the central features.

The impression of the new buildings should be in keeping with the industrial character of the area, with openings highlighting the rudimentary inner area. Materials contributing to that idea include unfinished formwork concrete, steel and opaque polycarbonate.

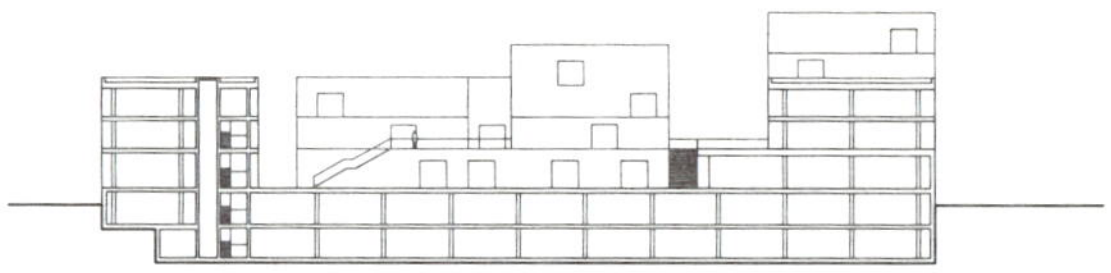

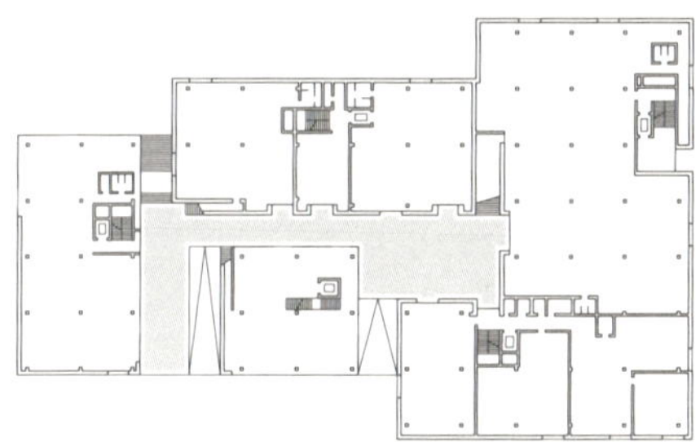

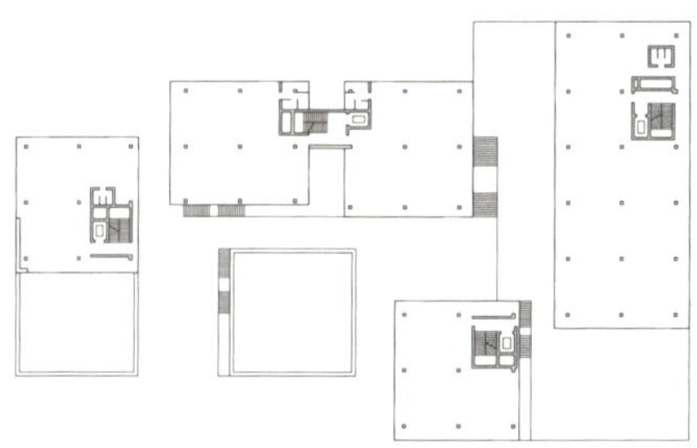

REBEL HOUSE

Take a small patch of land and make the most of it. Challenge accepted!

Architects | Atelier van Wengerden – Jacco van Wengerden, Gijs Baks, Milda Grabauskaite
Location | Homeruskwartier, Almere, The Netherlands
Completion | 2013
Size | 77 sqm

The available space measured 9x8 meters, with a permitted height of just 3.7 meters. Other tight parameters included a limited budget, proximity to the site boundaries and low maintenance. The possibilities of a detached house were maximized with views and light on all sides. Interesting features include indentations on the east and west façades, with one continuing in the roof, enabling an opening to the east and an entrance awning on the west side. The exterior is clad with corrugated aluminum sheeting. Not the obvious material for a residential project, but it has proven to be cost effective and robust. While the exterior is functional, the open plan interior is warm and timbered. A detached interior box houses the bathroom, cloakroom cupboard, cabinets, wardrobe and even a guest bed, with a sliding door to separate the living and sleeping areas.

In Almere, The Netherlands, parcels of land were made available for people to build their own homes. The small size of the plots represented an interesting challenge that was solved via an inspired use of light and materials.

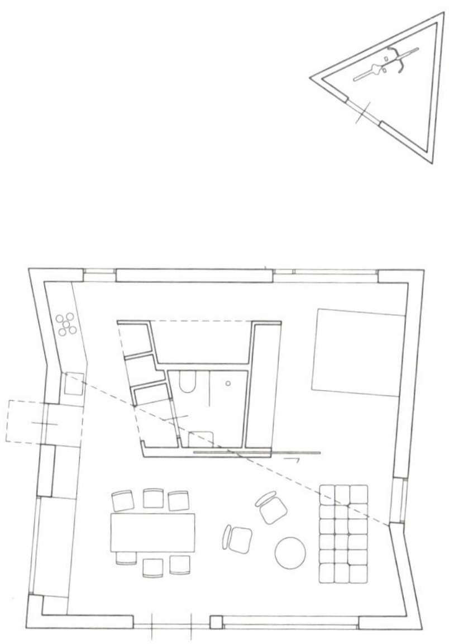

MEETING POINT, PLAN 09

Let's talk about architecture! Because inspiring architecture can inspire change!

Architects | LHVH ARCHITEKTEN
Location | Filzengraben 2, 50676 Cologne, Germany
Completion | 2009
Size | 28 sqm

This meeting point of an architecture event only transmits the idea of a building. A concrete formwork roughly describing an exterior extending into the future engages the fantasy of the viewer and becomes a multitude of different houses. The idea of constructing a simple hut from the yellow concrete formwork elements captures the gist of the makeshift. The concrete that will never be poured here is a fantasy material for creative spirits to shape for themselves. Detached from the physical body, the transcendent space will serve various purposes during the event. Seven days later the spirit flies away and the formwork will shape other buildings.

plan19

The archetype of a house develops from the curious color, but also from the associations with slum and favela buildings, narrative qualities which are capable of inspiring the process of talking about architecture.

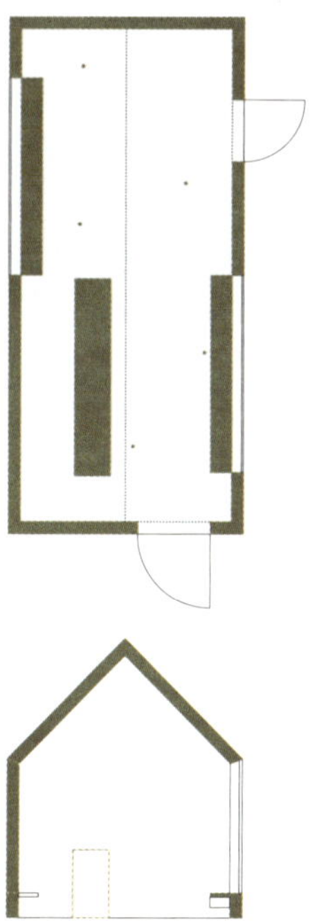

CAN FRAMIS MUSEUM

Opposites attract. Catalan art among the high-rises of Barcelona's business district.

Architects | BAAS architects
Location | 22nd District, Poble Nou, Barcelona, Spain
Completion | early 19th century / 2009
Size | 5,468 sqm
Original use | wool mill

This museum is located in the 22nd district of Barcelona, which is now a high-rise, heavily built-up area. Can Framis aimed to play on contrasts, with a surrounding garden providing a quiet breathing space. The main interest of the two buildings to be preserved lies in the contrast of their location, based on the former agricultural plan prior to the Cerdà plan. The project involved the restoration of two factory buildings and the construction of a new building to link the different entities. The three buildings form a courtyard where the main entrance is located. Outside, the lime mortar blends with the existing stonework and merges with the exposed concrete. The façade then becomes a collage of textures.

A deliberately old-style garden, where vegetation will play the leading role. A natural haven, a chunk of nature within the city, in clear contrast to the surroundings. A somewhat windswept look, hardly mapped out, with narrow and winding paths and metallic green street furniture which evokes the past, with a certain air of melancholy, in tune with the building. The garden, slightly sunken with dunes (waves) which screen it from street level, and its masses of flora.

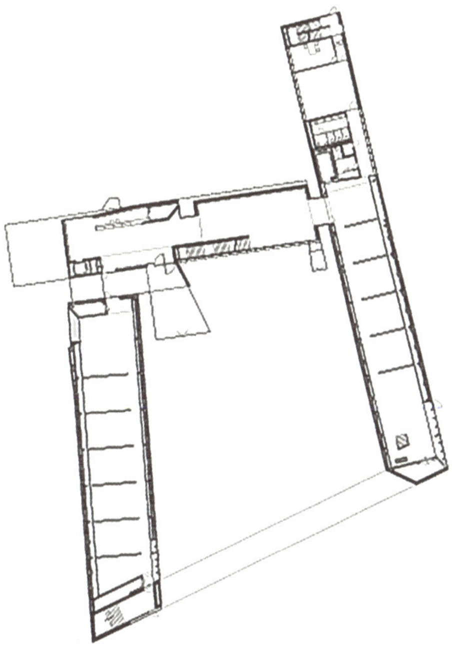

When their first daughter was born the young family had the idea of building their own one family house. They found a small house in need of renovation with a large yard in the Wienerwald. In order to achieve the space allocation it was necessary to build an additional two-story structure. Illumination of the partially below ground mother-in-law apartment on the ground floor is provided by ribbon windows that follow the course of the banister. A free-standing sanitation core subdivides the open space into bedroom and living room areas. Floating above the ground floor is the first expansion phase Wood Box. The children (now there are three) are now intensively using the 3.5-meter-high playroom replete with climbing wall, swing and soccer goal. All installations for a later division of the space into four single rooms have already been prepared.

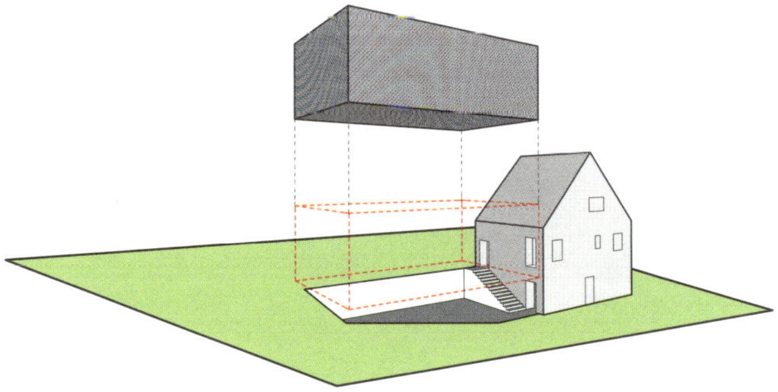

HEIMSPIEL EICHGRABEN

Multi generation. Multi-purpose. Conversion possible.

Architects | franz
Location | 3032 Eichgraben, Austria
Completion | 2012
Size | 420 sqm

The wooden box is built from massive wood slabs and is covered on all sides including the roof and nether side with diagonally running larch slats. Because of the complex geometry with a double miter cut, the gray stained slats were assembled by the employees of the architectural firm together with the client.

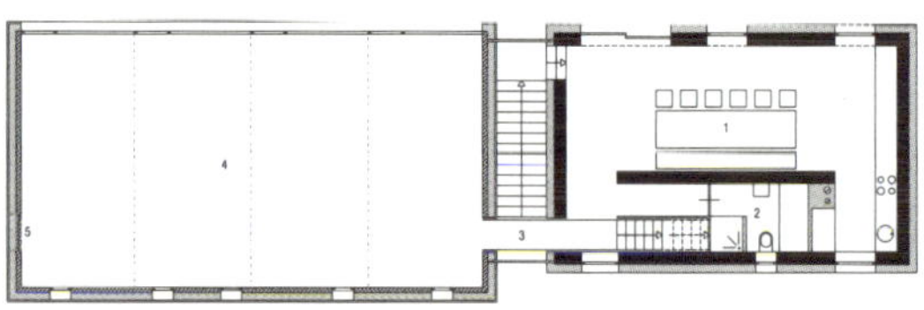

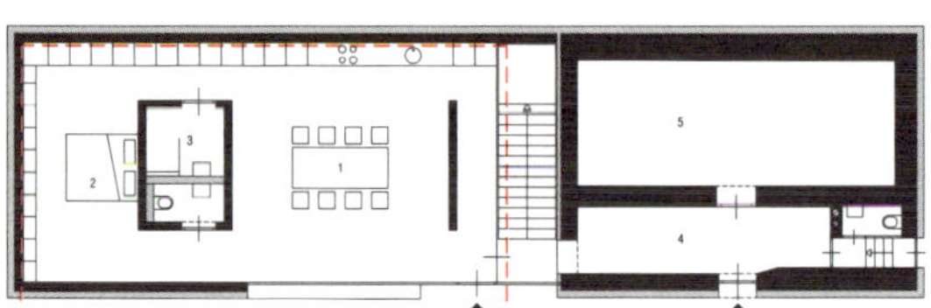

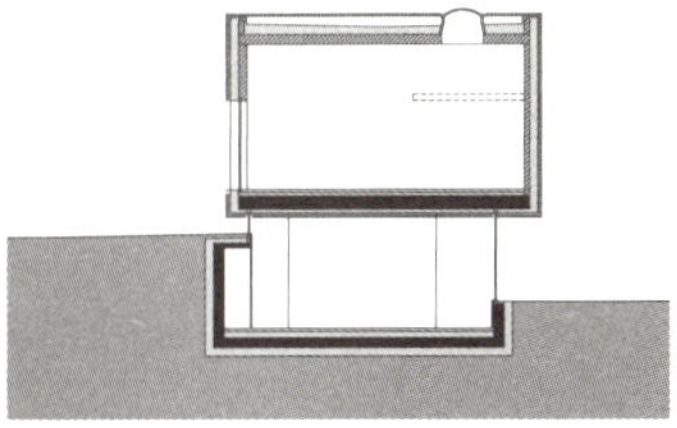

KEMENATE HAGENBRÜCKE

A survivor of many wars is finally able to tell its stories of yesteryear.

Architects | O.M. Architekten BDA – Rainer Ottinger, Thomas Möhlendick
Location | Hagenbrücke 5, 38100 Brunswick, Germany
Completion | 2nd half of the 13th century / 2015
Size | 266 sqm

The medieval bower is a stone building, the historical core of which was built on a framework ensemble and which granted the inhabitants security. After being destroyed in wartime, the building stood a long time alone. A sculptural and modern augmentation of the medieval monument adapts the historical embedding of the structure in a dense courtyard development. The result is a circular path through the museum with an improvement of use and experience of the rooms inside the building ensemble. The upper floor which can be used as a gallery is a closed cube with panorama windows on the narrow sides which define different views of the city.

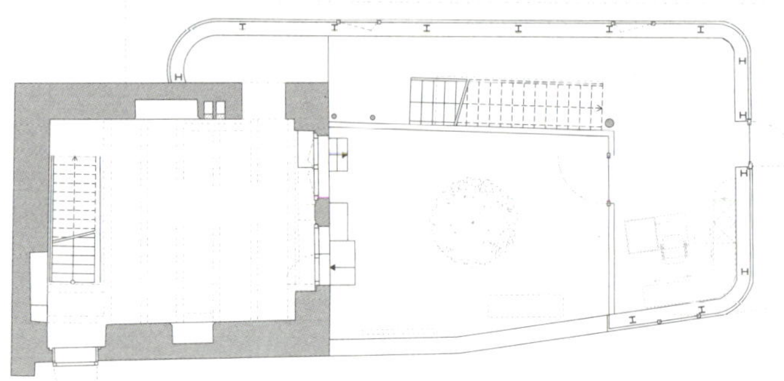

The Corten steel materiality which was selected for the addition recalls the Jakob Bower (Jakobs-Kapelle) ensemble which is also located in Brunswick. In the dialectic to the stone building it symbolizes the transience of the historic framework buildings.

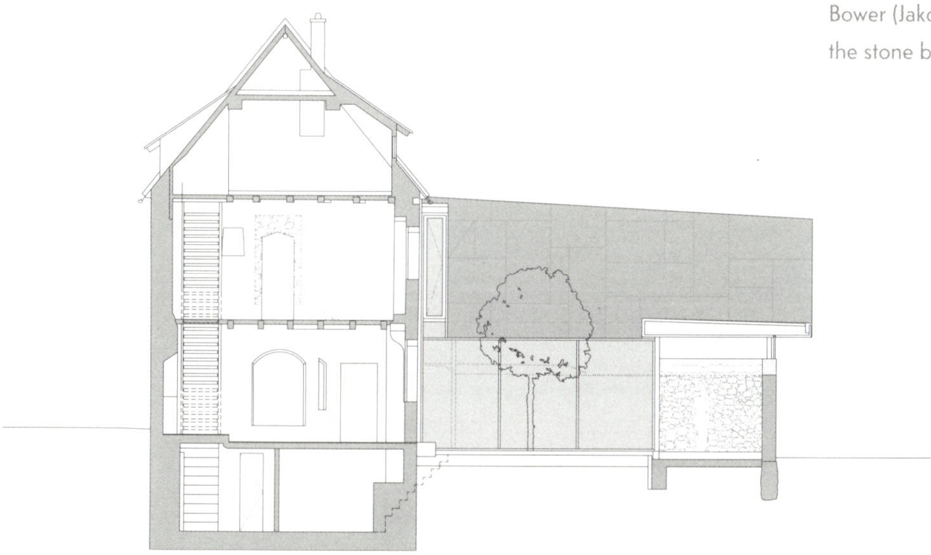

CASA MIGDIA

Everything is illuminated. Light was the beacon for this townhouse's design.

The project starts from two client's requirements for a house with plenty of natural light that can be increased in size through the years. To comply with those requirements SAU Taller de Arquitectura proposed a clear solution: to locate services and storage areas on the blank walls, leaving a central core to articulate the space around it. With this decision they free up the street and courtyard façades. Those façades are facing north and south so they can become a filter for light and ventilation. Another consequence of this decision is a flexible section which will allow future lightweight slabs to be built when the inhabitants want them. With this aim, concealed anchorages were left in the concrete to accommodate simple timber structures to be built in the future.

Architects | SAU taller d'arquitectura
Location | Migdia street, Granollers, Spain
Completion | 2014
Size | 173 sqm

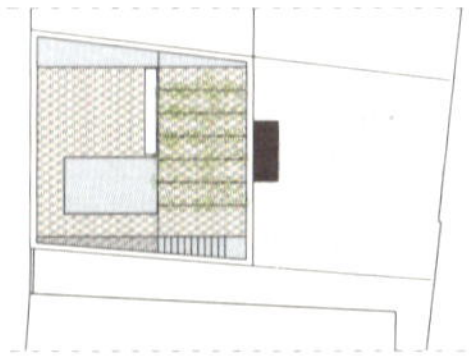

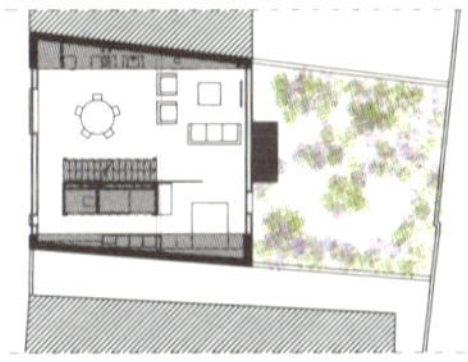

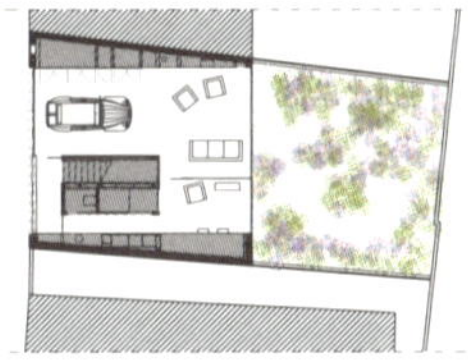

Façades had been thought of as a triple skin. They act as a filter to improve internal light, temperature and comfort conditions. The outer skin is made of 4 cm cellular polycarbonate and the inner one is made of double glass, with movable aluminum louvres located between the two layers. Facing south, there is the possibility to open or close the room between the polycarbonate and the glass depending on ventilation requirements. The house is designed for the best comfort using passive technologies.

WIESERGUT HOTEL

Mountain hut 2.0! Enjoy maximum comfort without missing that special rustic ambience during your skiing holiday.

Architects | Gogl Architekten – Monika Gogl
Location | Wiesern 48, 5754 Hinterglemm, Austria
Completion | 2012
Size | 5,544 sqm

The facility is fitted together from different structural typologies. The four story manor house operates as an ancient landmark. The one story lobby and one story garden suites integrated into the landscape together with the bathhouse tower in the south create an exciting building ensemble around the large garden. Far away from the tourist frenzy around it, the garden is a place of quiet and contemplation. The collage structure creates an interchange of exciting zones of light and shadow in reference to nature and retreat into the house. Native materials like oak and walnut, exposed concrete, natural stone, glass and wrought iron underscore the differentiated qualities of the space.

The Gogl Architekten team is also responsible for the interior design. In collaboration with regional manufacturers, Gogl Architekten designed and built most of the furniture especially for the building. Natural material also dominates the interior. In addition to linen and loden cloth, ceramic lamps, deerskin benches and wood furniture, there are also iron stoves.

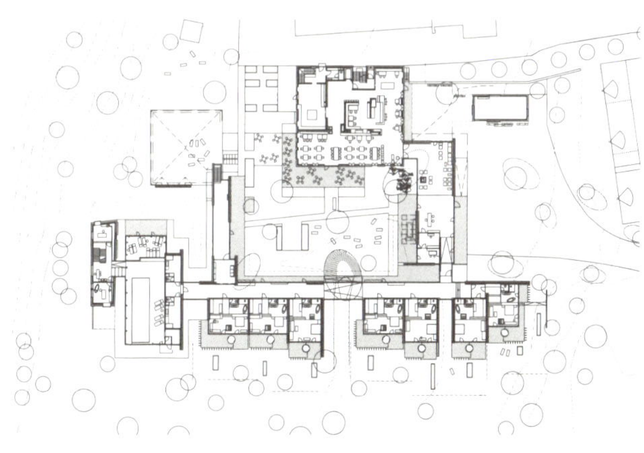

DINESEN SHOWROOM

Finest Danish craftsmanship showcased on 600 m².

Architects | OEO STUDIO
Location | Søtorvet 5, Copenhagen, Denmark
Completion | 2014
Size | 600 sqm

Dinesen has a strong passion for wood. Their showroom is divided in two sections which highlight Dinesen's bold new direction and showcase the perfect simplicity of the company's wood alongside new bespoke creations. One part takes the exclusiveness of long and wide wooden planks to a new level. It is like entering a private apartment with a ballroom and dining area, library and custom-made kitchen and wine cellar. The other part is an unfinished and playful universe, which presents a more creative Dinesen. The main gallery room has a unique and individualized look, featuring both a huge wooden structure playing with light and shadow as well as a reception area inspired by the new coffee culture found in the streets of Tokyo. A 15-meter-long plank table pulls the space together.

The design vision was to create a fully embracing spatial experience. What the architects seek is to inspire people to indulge themselves fully in the universe. They want people to think of Dinesen as offering so much more than perfect, immaculate flooring. They want to inspire people to think in new and different ways.

Architects | EMF – Estudi Martí Franch + Ardèvol consultors associats
Location | Cap de Creus, Catalunya, Spain
Completion | 2010
Size | 90 ha

TUDELA-CULIP RESTORATION PROJECT

The curtain has fallen. The days of Club Med are over. Now is the time for nature at Cap de Creus.

This project is a showcase for landscape-driven nature restoration projects. From a demolition order for habitat reclamation, it becomes a creative landscape restoration development. Operating within a tight budget, the design skillfully orchestrates the deconstruction as a combination of destruction and construction to bring out the site's peculiarities, both natural and cultural. By choreographing on-site visitors in a narrative that stimulates the culture in nature, an innovative approach emerges to answer the question of whether erasing and voiding is just as valid as filling in and adding.

During the five years process, the designers walked more than 200 kilometers on site, took and studied more than 15,000 pictures, and received up to 50 specialists in different fields related to nature restoration in their search for ways to optimize deconstruction, nature dynamic reclamation, and social valorization.

CULTURAL CENTER BRITZ

Fine dining in an oxen barn? Classical music in a cowshed? Once a farm, now a stage for culture!

Architects | Abelmann Vielain Pock Architects BDA
Location | Alt-Britz, Berlin-Neukölln, Germany
Completion | 2012
Size | 3.1 ha
Original use | cowshed, horse stable

The new "Kulturstall" with an open air stage is part of the new "Kulturzentrum Gutshof Britz" ensemble. New uses for the facility have been created in the former stalls, apartments and office spaces. They are: the "Paul Hindemith School of Music" in the estate administration house, the "Neukölln Museum" in the horse stable with smithy, a small ballroom for rent in the oxen stall, the restaurant in the "Schweizer Haus", and the theater and concert hall in the cow shed. The last building phase in 2011 saw the completion of the former cow shed with the adjacent open-air theater. In all of the new sections the architects have followed the idea of making the new uses clearly and contemporaneously legible while telling something about the history of the location, with its special features, former architectural functions and designs by means of a 'liberating' renaturation.

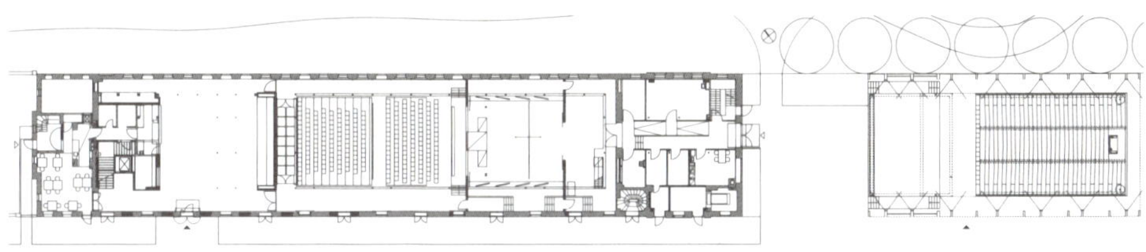

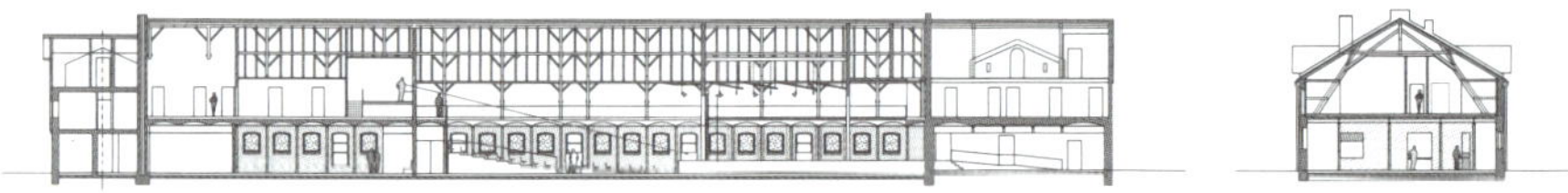

All construction elements, like exposed masonry inside and out, were tweaked, but are complemented or completed with similar materials. All interventions and additions were rigorously executed in colored exposed concrete unfinished formwork and color accentuated with glaze.

MOYAMOYA

A house with a studio skillfully wrapped around it shows that the art of Sushi making influences everything!

Architects | Fumihiko Sano / studio PHENOMENON
Location | Higashikurume, Tokyo, Japan
Completion | 2014
Size | 234 sqm

The studio lies in a suburb of Tokyo and was constructed around the center of the house. It is a place where the client can study and dye kimonos, her chief hobby and is a place of interaction and communication. The shape of the building plot is a square of 9.1 x 9.1 meters sloping to the north and south. Taking advantage of the slanting ground, a private space was located in the north commanding a fine view. An open ceiling studio is connected to a kitchen, allowing the client to hold a big party if she wants. In consideration of her aging, the bedroom, study and other infrastructures are on the first floor. Other single rooms, a living room, and a Japanese style room are on the second floor and there is a fine view of Mount Fuji from the living room.

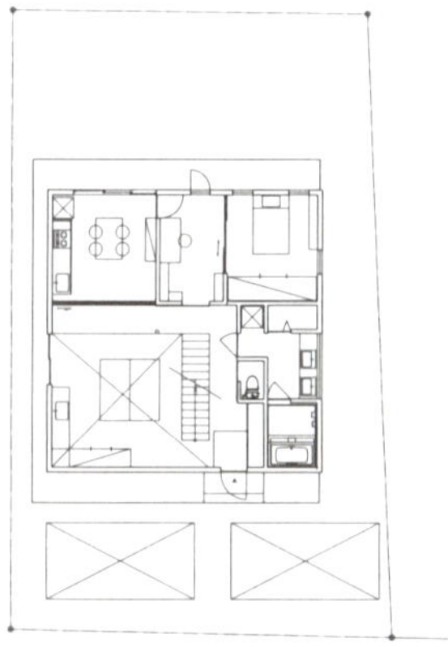

Being swayed by the wind, the stainless steel fence shines and causes a great variety of moire patterns. The angle and strength of the light change throughout the day, from morning, afternoon, evening, to night. The change of the light not only creates stirring moire patterns, but also gives different and diverse impressions to the house. This is the place where people can closely enjoy the transitions of time, seasons, and climates through the medium of the house.

COMMUNITY HALL MÄNNEDORF

Retain or replace, that was the question.
SAM opted for ... retention!

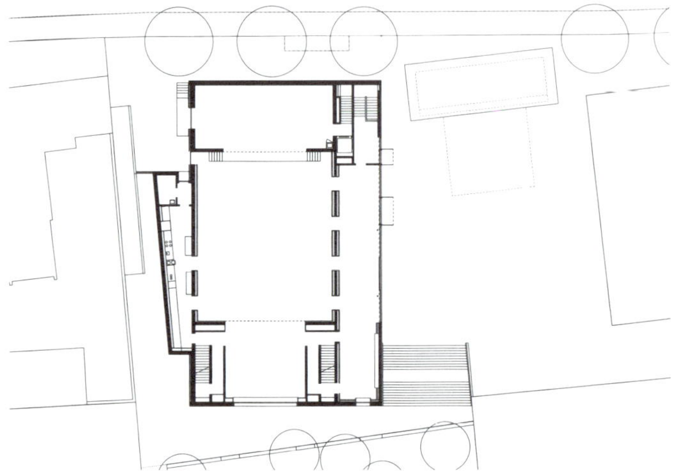

Architects | SAM Architects and Partner, Zurich, Switzerland
Location | Alte Landstrasse 250, Männedorf, Zurich, Switzerland
Completion | 1939 / 2011
Size | 1,860 sqm
Original use | church parish hall

The new community hall replaces the former church hall which had been used for meetings, it is built in the same location and offers additional space for meetings and events held by the clubs. The landscaped square on the lakeside of the building accesses the club rooms and is connected to the town square at a higher elevation via a flight of stairs. The completion of the community hall will constitute the keystone of the new Zentrum Leue. In addition to the form and exterior design the vine motifs are a reminder of local traditions which also reflect the needs of a modern parish.

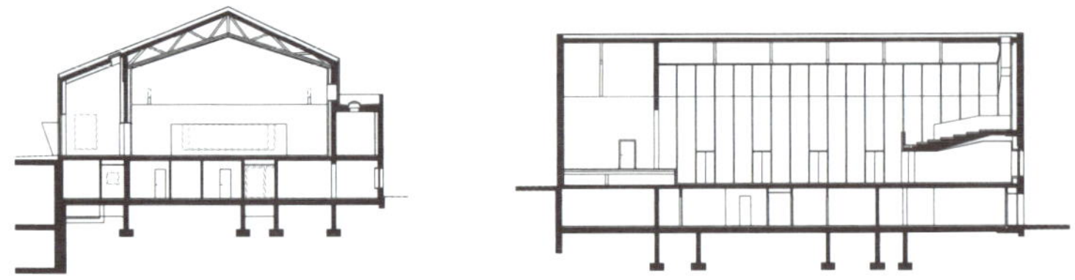

The outer form of the community hall resembles a marquee: expanded metal panels cover the roof and the façades like the fabric of a tent. Inside the lobby and the hall oak railings run like tent poles from the floor to beneath the gables. The oak slats and flooring and the grape motif printed on the wall paneling are reminders of the wine-making tradition of the village. The colored glass balls of the chandeliers also pick up the grape motif.

SAAL

Reformiertes Kirchgemeindehaus
GEMEINDESAAL

MAISON L

Mini skyscrapers tower up from shared living areas without losing the famous French sense of style.

Less than half an hour's drive west from Paris' city center, designed as an extension of a private residence to an 18th-century structure, the new building sought to provide every family member with a private realm. The roughly 5,000 square meters plot of old trees called for a project that would leave the spacious grounds predominantly untouched to ensure a minimal impact on the mature landscape. Due to local building codes five tower-like volumes have been employed. Positioned to frame a specific perspective of the site, each flat-roofed, eight-meters-high concrete 'tower' houses a dressing room and storage space, a bathroom and a bedroom. The design foresaw an amorphous plinth storey with curved stone walls heaped up with earth and used as a general living area. A completely 'superfluous' space without specific functional qualities.

Architects | christian pottgiesser architecturespossibles
Location | Yvelines, France
Completion | 2011
Size | 926 sqm

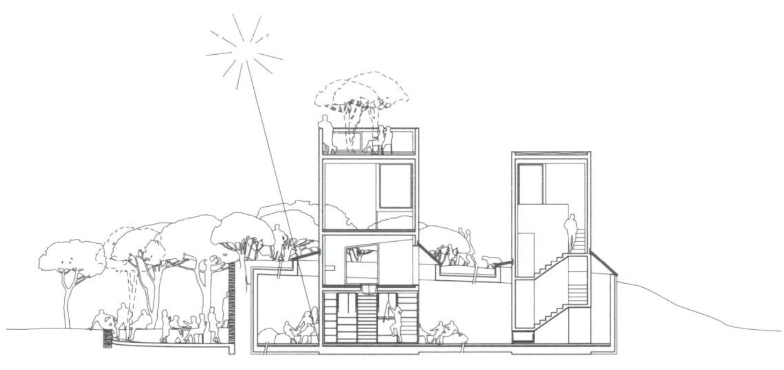

House and landscape are intimately interwoven, boundaries between indoors and outdoors are blurred. The south-eastern façade emerges from a complex topography between the house and its landscape. The river-bed-shaped, undulating terrain distorts, blending the construction into nature.

WILDLIFE OBSERVATION PAVILION

Camouflage is everything. Enjoy nature from up close without disturbing the animal kingdom.

Architects | Morscher Architekten
Location | Tierparkweg 3d, 3005 Bern, Switzerland
Completion | 2013
Size | 143 sqm

The form and location of the new wildlife observation pavilion in the Bern zoo is marked by its placement between old trees and existing enclosures. A golden green, hide-like mosaic façade clings to the outer walls and the roof while in keeping with the metaphor the interior is dark red. Large, gold-colored observation frames open up to the forest and the enclosures. The multi-purpose covered shelter is used for jazz matinees and barbeques for the zoo visitors, but also serves as a protected observation point for watching wolves, marmots and small mammals. A rest room facility for families and the handicapped which is easy to reach for all zoo visitors on the main parking promenade fills out the pavilion.

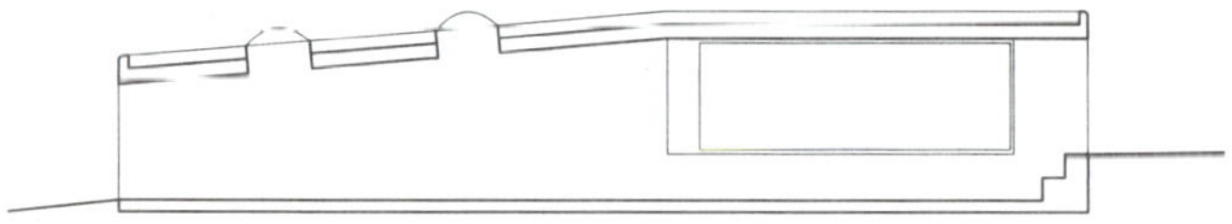

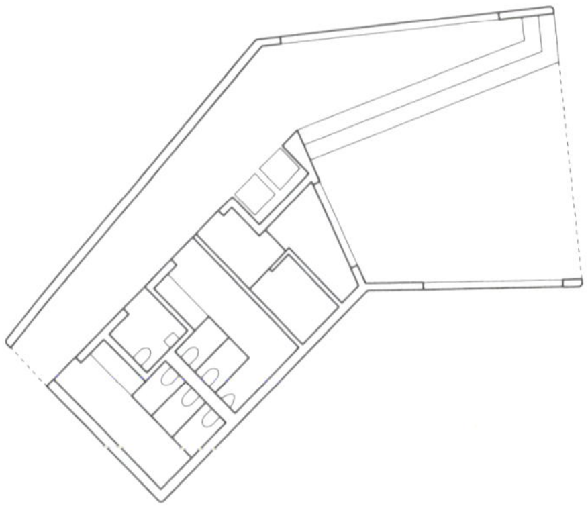

CHAPEL RESTORATION

Love all, serve all. Reflecting back on Christian values, this sanctuary provides space for everyone.

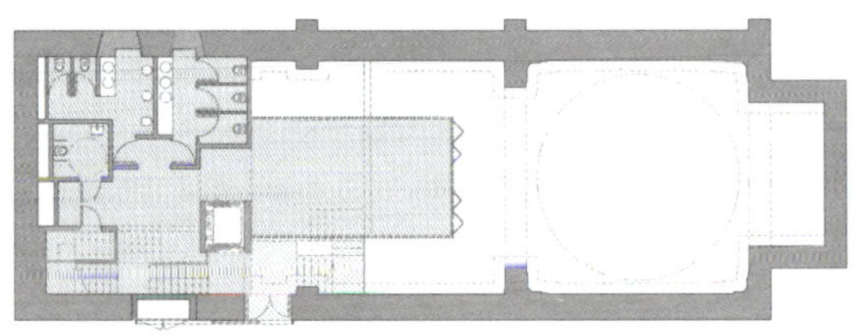

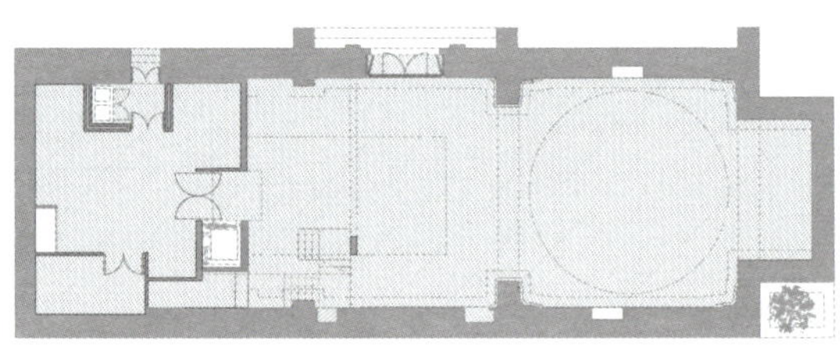

The chapel rehabilitation created a new typology — a multi-purpose space for events — ranging from a formal wedding to the mellow ambiance of a yoga retreat. The restart involved resolving the complex pathologies suffered by the original structure since it was abandoned in 1969. Adam Bresnick architects studied and restored the existing architecture as well as inserting new uses. The philosophy guiding the intervention was to respect the passing of time. The stone façades were repointed, traditional tile eaves restored and stone moldings were left with their worn faults, including the original scarred Serlian entrance. In the interior three distinct areas are articulated, the refurbished dome where the original space is restored, the entrance into the nave with a mix of archaeological remains and a new construction cantilevered over the space, minimally touching the original.

Architects | Adam Bresnick architects
Location | Avenida de la Constitución 4, Brihuega, Guadalajara, 19400 Spain
Completion | 16th century / 2013
Size | 507 sqm
Original use | chapel

The materials used are the same as the original; beige marble main floor, upper levels in black resin, white paint on the plaster moldings and pine slats on the ceiling which enclose the modern choir floating within the volume of the nave.

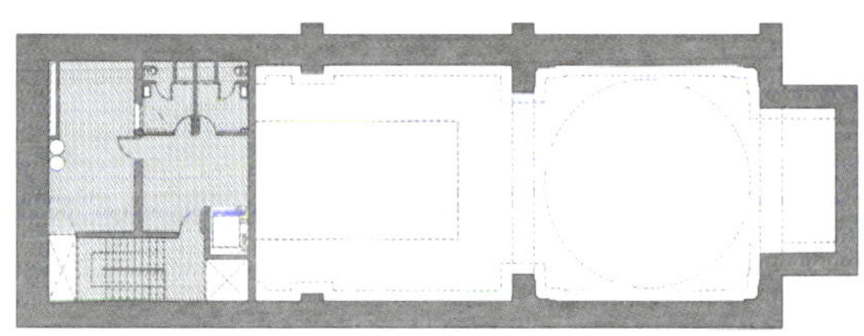

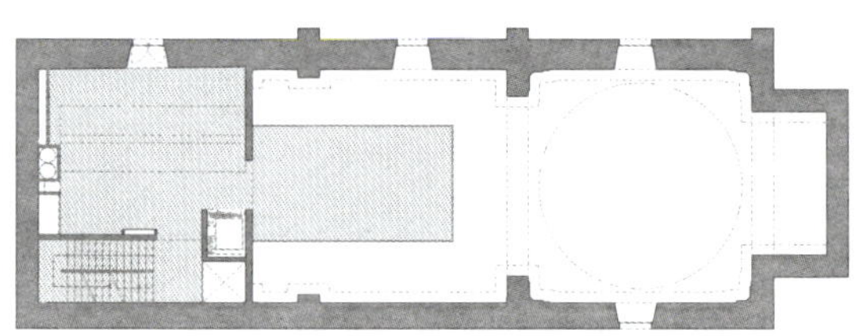

THOMMY HOUSE

Clear the stage for ... concrete!

Architects | Nissen & Wentzlaff Architekten BSA SIA AG
Location | 4103 Bottmingen, Switzerland
Completion | 2011
Size | 150 sqm

The arrangement of different building blocks, including a residence, swimming pond, an outbuilding and enclosure wall, creates an ensemble played out over the entire property. The old stock of trees makes the contact with the property. The enclosure wall leads the visitor to the access in the east. With an east-west orientation, the house is placed over the basement of the predecessor house. In order to underscore the minimalist design, the windows on each side are grouped in a window front. Large scale interactions between the inside and outside develop in all directions.

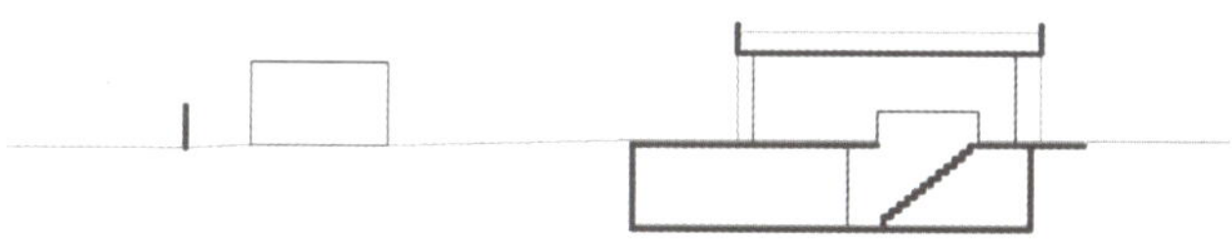

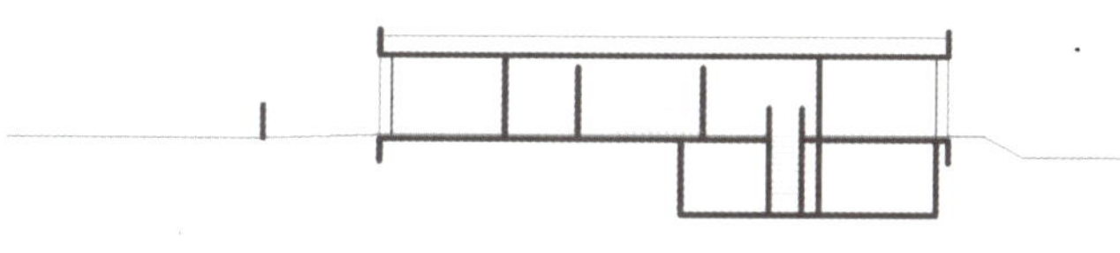

To underscore the monolithic impression of the residence, the outer shell was made of colored insulating concrete. The characteristics of this material, including irregular pockets of air and color gradients were consciously selected to liven up and lend structure to the façade surfaces.

SZ-HK BIENNALE SILO RECONVERSION

Silo revamped. Let yourself be drawn into a spiral of spatial sensation.

The silo building is composed of three parts in the plan: two thin steel silos 5.4 meters in diameter at the west end, four concrete silos 14 meters in diameter in the middle, and at the east end, a rectangular vertical transportation tower. In elevation, the building is also composed of three parts: a 6-meter-high discharging level on the ground, six 30-meter-high silos shaping the main buildings in the middle, and on top, a 3.6-meter-high horizontal material-inlet level. A unique spatial detour routine was implanted in the gigantic functional artefact. Weightless, transparent and abstract spatial installations were implanted in the empty background after the shutdown of industrial function. Bridges, ramps, staircases and walls were built to articulate the breakthroughs and intervals of the original space.

Architects | O-office Architects
Location | Haiwan Road, Nanshan District, Shezhen, China
Completion | 1987 / 2013
Size | 2,662 sqm
Original use | storage silos for rough materials of glass production

Conservation of architecture is not only a matter of preserving history and physical space and it is more than just recycling old buildings for new functions. The conversion of the former Guangdong Floating Glass Factory is an experiment of rediscovering the lost spatial existence and experience via the architectural study of contemporary industrial relics, which were expected to unveil a new architectural design and urban approach for contemporary Chinese cities.

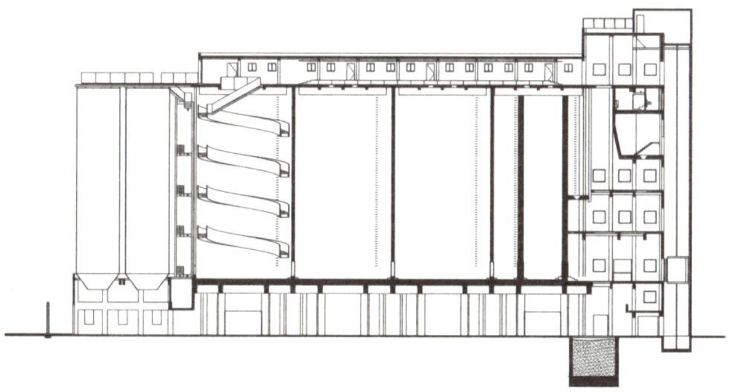

BOCHUM PUMP HOUSE

Remodel a former industrial building and get an almost abstract archetype of a house with a saddle roof.

The former Bochumer Verein pump station is in the immediate vicinity of the Jahrhunderthalle, the central venue of the Ruhr Triennale. The design is a reaction to the already established ensemble of heterogeneous old inventory and augmented by new construction. A new climate envelope which fulfills the demands of insulation was slipped over the existing building, an open hall with a façade made of masonry filled steel framework. The impression in the interior created by the signs of wear and the filigree roof trusses could thereby be retained. An inserted box for the washroom separates the two use areas, the visitors' center and the restaurant. This makes it possible to operate the two functional areas independently. The guest room is characterized by the historical elements.

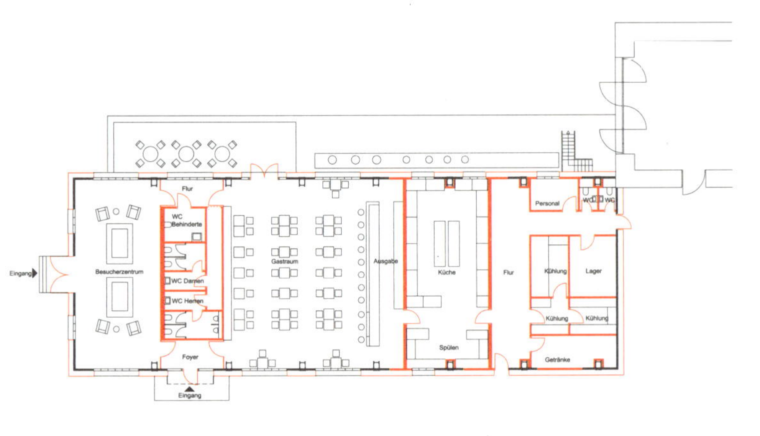

Architects | Heinrich Böll Architekt BDA DWB
Client | NRW.Urban, Dortmund
Location | An der Jahrhunderthalle 1, 44793 Bochum, Germany
Completion | ca. 1900 / 2012
Size | 1,200 sqm
Original use | pump house

The architects pursue the approach of slipping a new outer envelope over the building volume. Although the old façade loses its role as a climate moderator, it can be retained almost unchanged, with partially repaired sections that have been severely damaged due to corrosion. The atmosphere in the interior is marked by the untreated wall surfaces, creating a striking contrast between the reduced form language of the house and the surroundings of relicts from the former steel production.

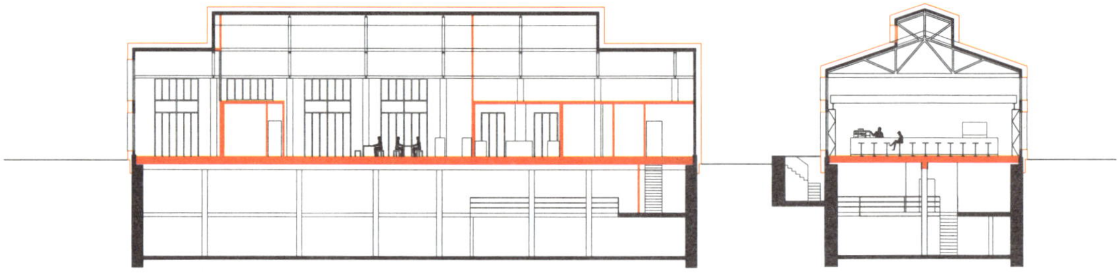

LEESON PARK

Georgian style complemented perfectly by state-of-the-art technology.

Architects | ODKM Architects
Location | South Dublin, Ireland
Completion | 2012
Size | 45 sqm (additional)
Origina use | derelict Georgian property

This project completely transformed a derelict Georgian property in Dublin. The architects dropped the entire ground floor level throughout and to the rear and brought the angled stone boundary wall which was a feature of the site into the heart of the house. An angled glazed bench seat forms the dining space which helped preserve the original form and footprint of the house. Corten steel cladding envelopes the projection to the rear which will change and grow with the house in the years to come, weathering as a beautiful counterpoint to the stone wall.

Architects | SUPPOSE DESIGN OFFICE
Location | Hiroshima, Japan
Completion | 2012
Size | 112 sqm

The idea of the house is an incomplete / complete form. Unlike other projects, the final stage of construction was not a finished state, but was left to let the owner experience the sense of completion by living here. The house interior is designed to maximize the interaction with its surroundings. The ground retained a tree standing in the center to provide a natural contrast with the surroundings. First story windows are kept open and create an interesting interaction with wind and rain. All these elements enhance the experience of unlimited lifestyle that is potentially contained in the house, minimizing boundaries. Through this different interpretation of connecting the exterior and interior space, new ways of living can be explored by the client.

HOUSE IN YAGI

Shell construction meets bungalow. At first glance, there is barely a sign of inhabitants.

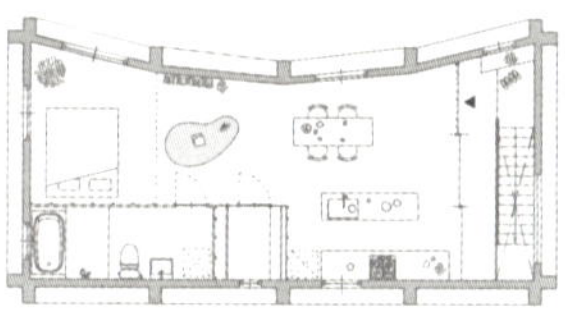

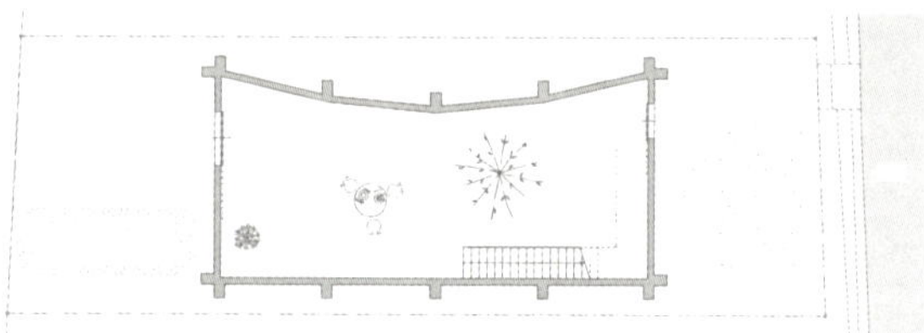

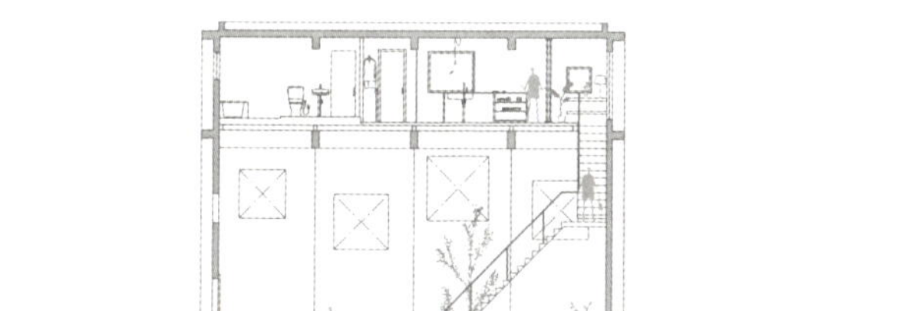

EDUCATION CENTER OBERES SCHLOSS

Multifunctional since 1518. This is why preservation came first.

The municipal reorientation of the Schlossplatz was the opening shot in the extensive new design of the Neuhausen center. In addition, the reorientation of the public spaces was an important building block in the revitalization of the listed upper castle. In order to create visual connections between the Kirchplatz, Schlossplatz and the Ochsengarten, the listed castle, built in 1518, was exposed by demolishing modern buildings around it. A new stairway was established in front of the Schlossplatz and the previously closed portal was reopened. The new, longitudinal glazed staircase guarantees the independent usage in the individual floors and offers views into the center of the city. A detailed dialogue between renovation and preservation significantly characterized the process, from design to planning.

Architects | Cheret Bozic Architekten
Location | Schlossplatz 7, 73761 Neuhausen auf den Fildern, Germany
Completion | 1518 / 2011
Size | 1,500 sqm
Original use | residence and representation building of a noble dynasty

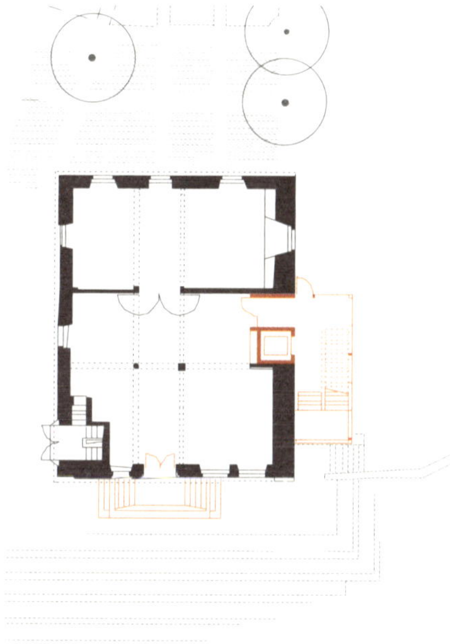

The renovation of the timber framing and the strengthening of the load-bearing structure required extensive structural interventions and measures which were demanding from a historical preservation standpoint. The informed involvement of a community with their public spaces was notable, including the discussion about the architectural identity of the location and the courage to invest in the project. The lively urbanity that developed in the context of the change in the town center was the delightful result.

THE DELI COUNTER

A delicious lunch enjoyed in an industrial chic setting – the perfect ingredients for a time-out from the bustling world outside.

Architects | Yaron Kanor, Dana Goldberg / studioY
Location | 211–213 Queen Street, Melbourne, VIC, Australia
Completion | 2014
Size | 140 sqm

The Deli Counter was brought to life by StudioY — a Melbourne firm with a track record of excellent urban hospitality fit outs. As a contemporary re-imagining of classic deli-style eateries, its design honors and enhances the historic space. The dramatic entryway — an artefact from the building's early days — screams with urban energy. Stripped-back architecture, salvaged objects and utilitarian surfaces conjure a warm, rustic atmosphere. Blue and white tiles in the kitchen are clean and classy, while the red, white and blue detailing across the café walls add graphic flair. It's idiosyncratic but pared back, allowing the genuine deli experience to be the hero. It's down-to-earth and old-school — and all the more modern and chic for it.

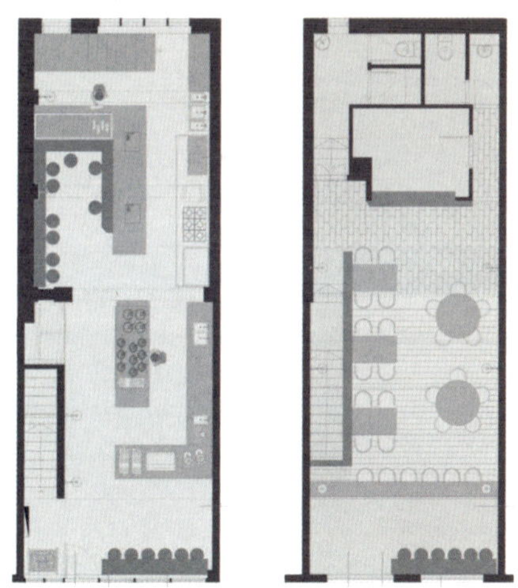

Creating warm, comforting atmosphere amid the din of the city was studioY's key goal design for The Deli Counter. Removing part of the first floor opened up a full-height expanse at the front of the venue, loosening diners' shoulders and letting in oodles of light. Timber from the first floor has been recast as shop-counter tops. Shelves and counters are constructed from robust, non-uniform crates. Brick walls have been exposed and other parts painted white to enhance natural light.

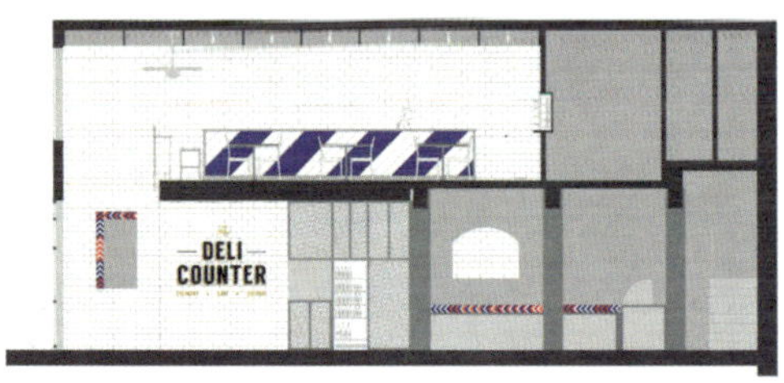

SUPERIOR QUALITY

HIŽA

Back to the roots. An homage to Croatian building tradition.

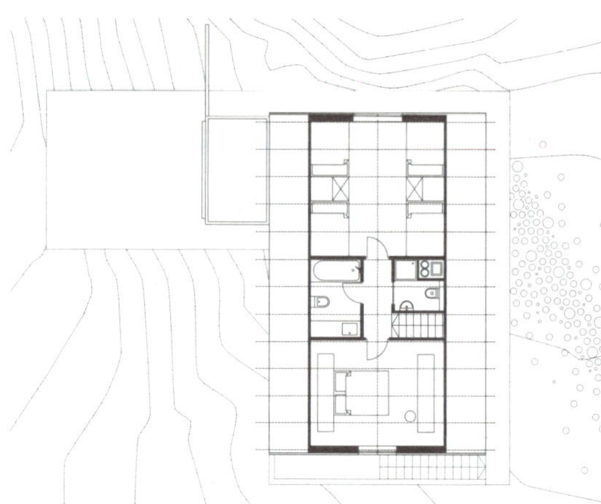

Architects | PROARH / Davor Matekovic
Collaborating architect | Oskar Rajko
Location | Kumrovec, Croatia
Completion | 1880 / 2012
Size | 230 sqm

The pre-existing traditional Zagorje cottage was structurally and statically in poor condition and was renovated in consideration of local heritage and design. The house form is kept, while the porch is substituted by a glass cube. To give the cottage southern exposure, the glass form slides out from the main volume, simultaneously forming an entrance area. Ground floor spaces are arranged following a traditional system of organization that creates a common zone with the 'hearth'. The straw covering on the roof is replaced with a new one which extends over the façade, while the gables are newly wood-covered. The entrance walkway is made of tree stumps. The existing stone pedestal is kept, while the newly designed terrace features wooden flooring and opens up to an impressive Zagorje landscape.

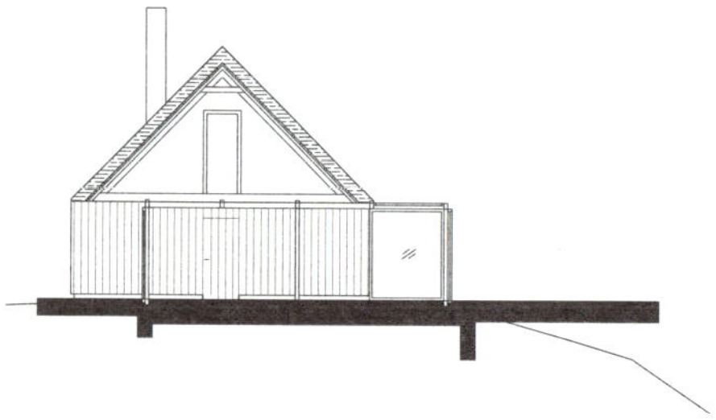

HIŽA is a contemporary interpretation of a traditional Zagorje cottage. The innovative use of straw, an archaic and forgotten material, on both roof and walls and wooden plank bearing construction, makes this house a subtle yet exuberant homage to the cultural heritage of the Zagorje region. As such the 'organic' cottage is easily renovated from locally available resources and workmanship. It breathes and changes with time, creating a healthy living environment.

NAMHAE CHEO-MA HOUSE

Layered look instead of renovation. Perhaps even a role model for the fashion industry?

Namhae Cheo-ma House is a project that was interpreted as a layered oriental theme defined by an easily available aluminum landscaping fence. Diamond shaped louvers create a modern interpretation of the traditional Cheo-ma line. Cheo-ma lines asymmetrically condense the energy while resetting the relationship between mankind and nature. The aluminum frame gives the form depth and creates stacked layers by dividing the space and forming a new layer. This is a new interpretation of the approach seen in traditional space in Korea.

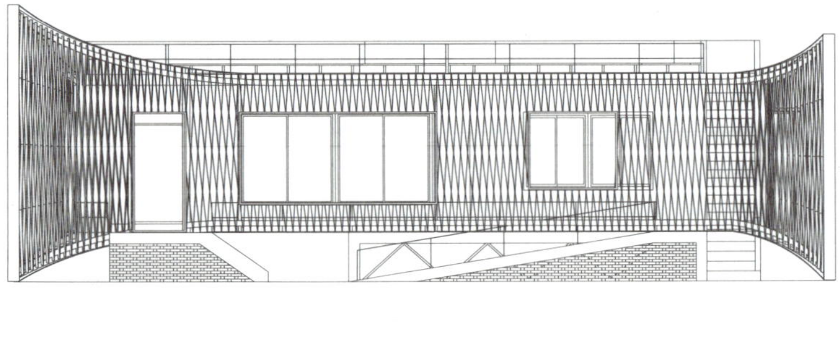

Architects | Jeonghoon Lee (Joho Architecture)
Location | 557-2 Namyang-ri, Seolcheon-myeon, Namhae-gun, Gyeongsangnamdo, Korea
Completion | 2011
Size | 105 sqm

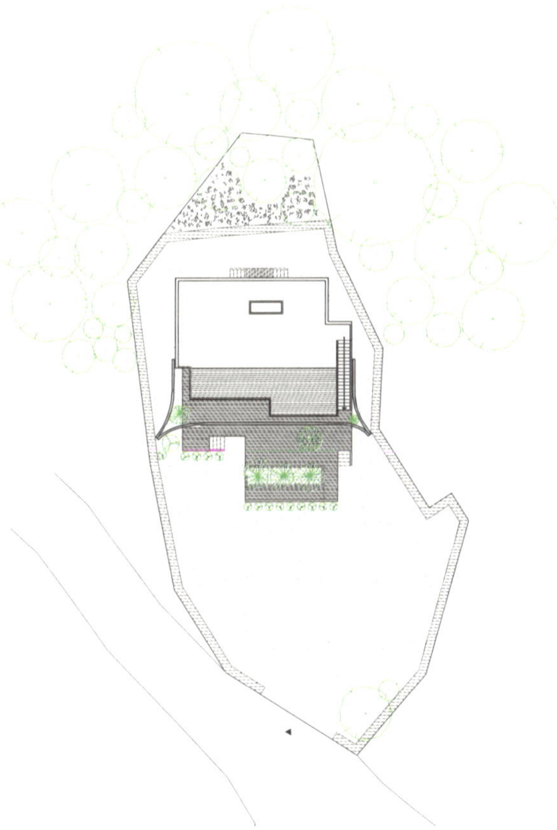

Cheo-ma is a human beings' imaginary action about nature and sky and a response to the beauty of the topography.

OCAÑA

Oldic but Goldic. A former factory space got in touch with its opulent side.

The Ocaña building is 150 years old, a space where radically different projects have been realized throughout the decades. A space in the very heart of Barcelona, shaped by the history and life of generations. Three parcels of three stores each, separated until now, have been connected to lend the ensemble strength and singularity. The result is a labyrinth, a wish fulfilled at every step, in which every glance discovers a new corner, a new astonishing angle. Ocaña now hosts four different spaces including two restaurants and two bars. The basic concept has been to respect the existing substance, discovering its beauty and rediscovering the 19th century architectural emphasis of handcraft which is too little appreciated today. Mission accomplished: the dignity of the Plaça Reial has been restored, conceived as an homage to the details.

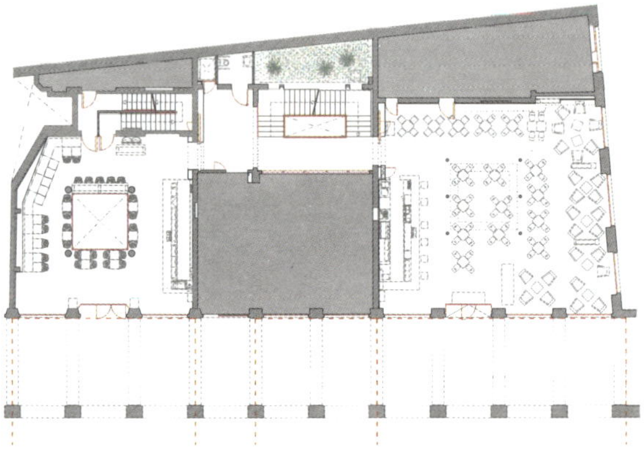

Design | Joaquina Laguna
Lighting designer | Odile Soudant
Location | Plaça Reial 13–15, 08002 Barcelona, Spain
Completion | 19th century / 2012
Size | 1,200 sqm
Original use | leather goods factory, clothing store, seals factory

The creators of Ocaña are passionate about antiques. Vintage furniture was brought from all over the world with an interior design that maintains the original structure of the building. They worked hard to recover and restore the original materials, including the café's European oak floor, whose complex plank by plank restoration process took over a year.

JAKOB-KEMENATE

Always wanted to feel like a fair maiden or a brave knight from the Middle Ages? You've come to the right place!

A new, modern two-and-a-half story structure with gable roof for the restoration of the bower in the urban development ensemble, with front building and Jakobs-Kapelle, will be located on the Jakobsstraße side. The new building will assume the profile of the historic front building, creating a spatial arrangement that recalls the original situation with the old church courtyard. The new ensemble will be created from the interplay between the Jakobs-Kapelle and the community center. The new construction steps should be legible in the historical chronology which is set off with a modern architectural language from the old building. A glazed lobby will be placed between the historical bower and the new building, from which point the connection and dialectic between old and new can be discerned. The entire ensemble will be used as an inner-city coaching and event complex. The new front building will be used as an apartment.

Architects | O.M. Architekten BDA — Rainer Ottinger, Thomas Möhlendick
Artist | Jörg Plickat
Location | Eiermarkt 1A, 38100 Brunswick, Germany
Completion | 1250 / 2006
Size | 439 sqm

Corten steel panels of different sizes are planned for the new façades and roof surfaces. The mosaic-like fabric will be assembled by hand by an artist which together with window formats of varying sizes and arrangements will orient to the predecessor building.

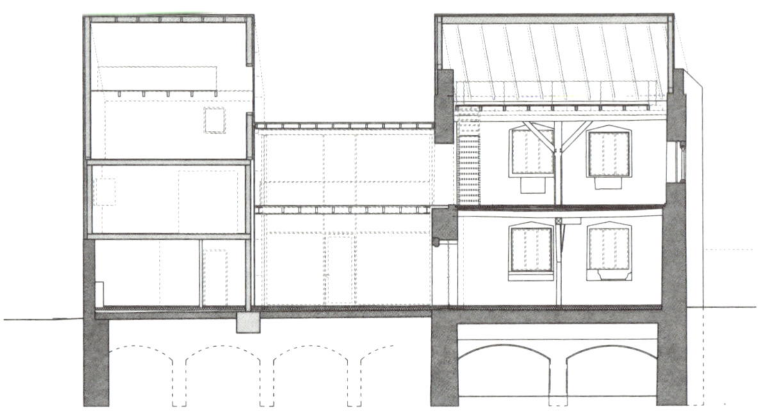

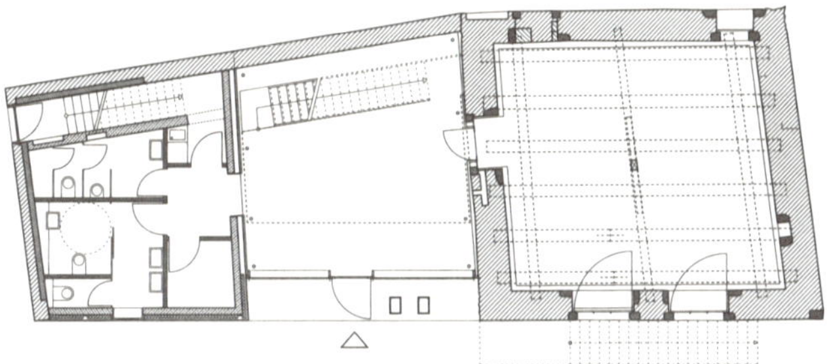

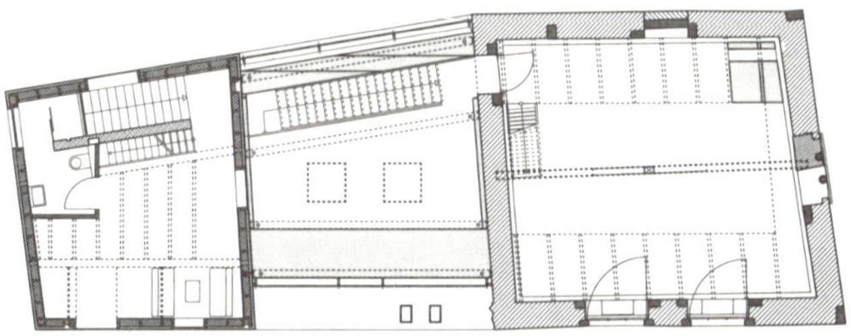

BLUE TAMAGAWA OUTDOOR FITNESS CLUB

Hard shell – soft core. Don't let it put you off. Behind the sober aluminum façade, a warm interior welcomes you.

Architects | frame design co.,ltd
Location | Komae, Tokyo, Japan
Completion | 2012
Size | 497 sqm

The surface railway has disappeared recently in Tokyo. It is now elevated on large concrete supports. This architecture helps pedestrians avoid traffic congestion via the railroad crossing and eases the movement of automobiles below. In contrast, the purpose of 'outdoor fitness' is to provide people with physical and mental health amenities. They can escape day-to-day stress with recreational activity. The designers have fused the two goals into a rich and natural environment that fulfils this program, whereby the building becomes a place for people to take a break from the work day and communicate with each other.

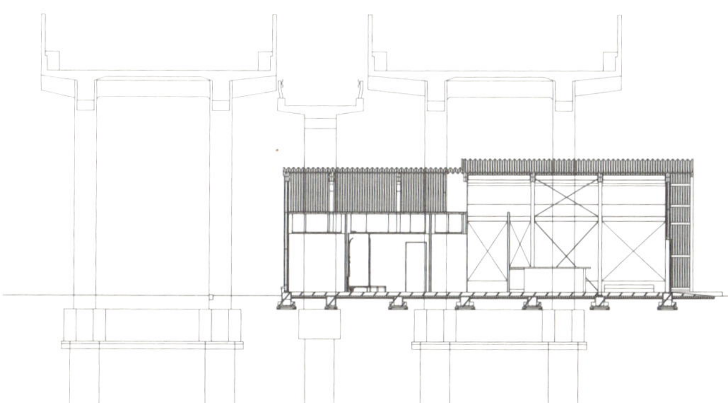

The iron frames and concrete pillars are in the room to support the special activity. Wooden floors convey warmth to the studio and terrace outside. The front-side corrugated steel panels set off the architecture from the concrete structure.

BLUE

LIBRE
patagonia

LOWE CAMPBELL EWALD HEADQUARTERS

The sky is the limit! Lots of space for lots of good ideas, all around an atrium unlike any other in Detroit.

Architects | Neumann/Smith Architecture
Location | Detroit, Michigan, USA
Completion | 1920 / 2014
Size | 11,334 sqm
Original use | former J.L. Hudson Co. warehouse

A creative space for a creative company. Lowe Campbell Ewald has breathed new life into a 100-year-old building, setting a precedent for the historic preservation of long vacant Detroit buildings and anchoring the creative sector's place as a strong economic engine for Detroit. Minimal fixed rooms create an open and collaborative office environment. The design makes creative use of recycled materials including wooden pallets, locally salvaged wood doors sliced up into slatted partition pods, and electrical conduits used as room dividers.

A five-story atrium and four-story LED screen with the ability to add customized messaging and imagery provides visual impact and serves as a key architectural feature. Neumann/Smith Architecture designed the screen to fill the height of the atrium and create a WOW-factor. The 42-foot-high display screen engages visitors and employees from the third floor atrium, which is designed as tiered platforms for private and company gatherings.

ANTONIO GALA PUBLIC LIBRARY

Bookshelf XXL. A reminiscence of the building's existing furniture.

Architects | Francisco López + Gudula Rudolf (Diputación Córdoba)
Location | Place María Auxiliadora s/n., Guadalcázar (Córdoba), Spain
Completion | 2011
Size | 409 sqm

The library, located opposite the Town Hall, was designed as a compact, concrete block, seven meters high, resting on its rear wall overlooking the front garden and the Town Hall building. The interior comprises a single space subdivided into two rooms placed one above the other. Though similar in layout, they offer a marked contrast in volume: while the ground-floor space is double height, thus conveying the impression of a large entrance hall, the upper floor has a more private feeling, its height being compressed to force a horizontal view of the garden. This division is achieved by means of an L-shaped wooden block which supports the staircase and conceals the necessary amenities.

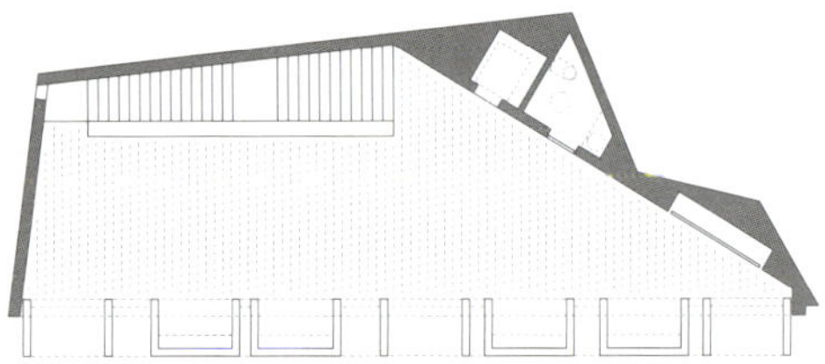

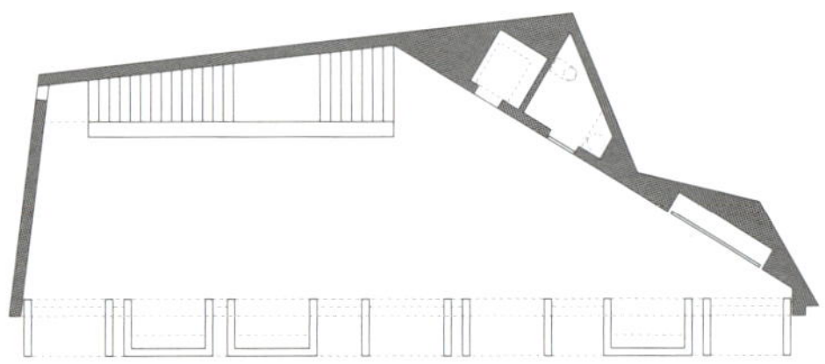

The essential element is the façade, a frontage built with a set of precast concrete frames manufactured in a neighboring village. This gives rise to a thick, alternating blind-open façade which shapes views while catering to functional needs. In doing so, it covers in one stroke the requirements of the project as a whole: a load-bearing façade which houses bookshelves, affords protection from sunlight, projects the view towards the garden, and achieves an overall qualitative impact.

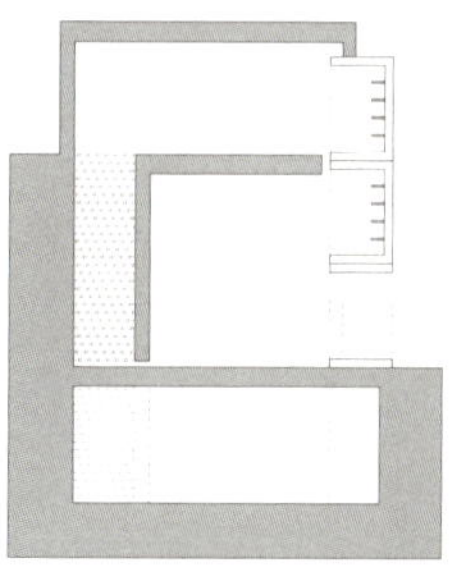
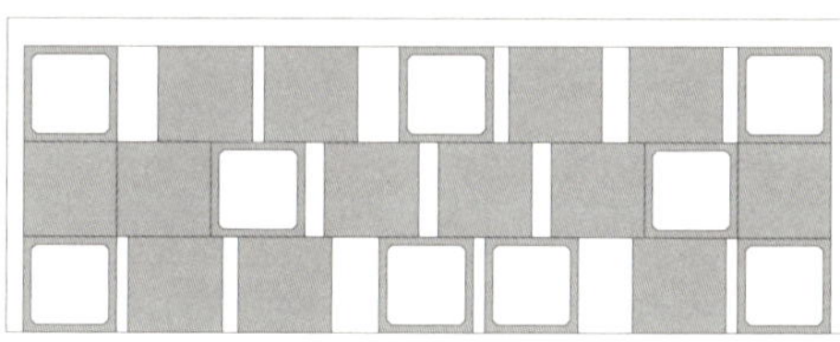

HET BURO / DE BOVENKAMER

Architectural archeology. This is where all time layers of the building as well as new ideas are uncovered.

Architects | Krill O.R.C.A – Christian Müller Architects
Location | Rochussenstraat, Rotterdam, The Netherlands
Completion | 2012
Size | 1,385 sqm

Het Buro/De Bovenkamer is a project developed and designed for young people. 24 studios have been realised in the Bovenkamer, twelve of which are for former drop-outs, who receive a few hours of professional guidance a week, while the other 12 are for young professionals acting as role models. With 475 square meters of office space the Buro provides small enterprises with the opportunity to start-up. The glazed corner will serve as a coffee corner, a meeting place for the youth, entrepreneurs from the Buro and people from the neighborhood. Ten apartments and a shop on the corner of Duysstraat and Rochussenstraat in Rotterdam West have been combined, transformed and sustainably enriched to serve this goal. Because the building is a municipal monument, the architects used both restoration techniques and modern detailing.

Krill/Christian Müller Architects decided to take an archaeological approach by re-exposing the time layers in the building. In addition to the architectural-cultural layer, the used material and traces of human intervention, in the form of notes drawn with pencil by the original builders on previously covered beams, the traces of black coal on the walls where the chimneys were removed, to the new Corten steel roof additions with structural glazing are all treated as part of the municipal monument.

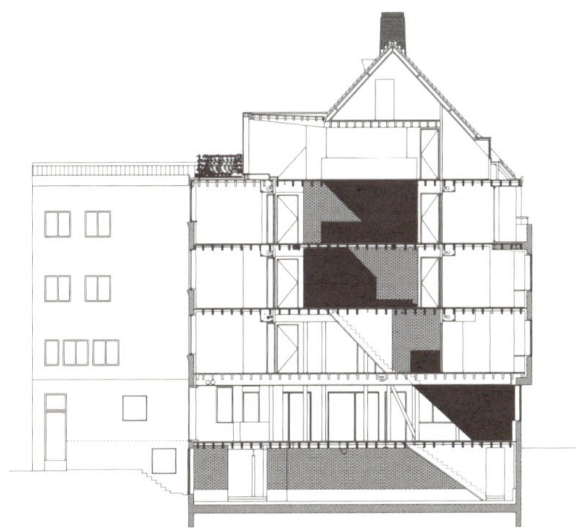

M03

Metal is the new brick. It will literally sparkle up your life

Architects | BAST
Location | Rue de la briqueterie, Toulouse, France
Completion | 2013
Size | 120 sqm

This construction reinterprets the house typology in the Toulousan suburb landscape in the character of the Brickyard street. In contrast with the preserved built base, the texture of which is highlighted by a distemper of lime, the new construction, a metallic light skeleton, aims towards abstraction. The new profile takes advantage of the light of the north. In the tradition of this street, the existing base and the new metallic construction develops housing environment typologies to answer current problems of urban renewal and the adaptation of the old to respond to new modes of life.

BS-528-RW

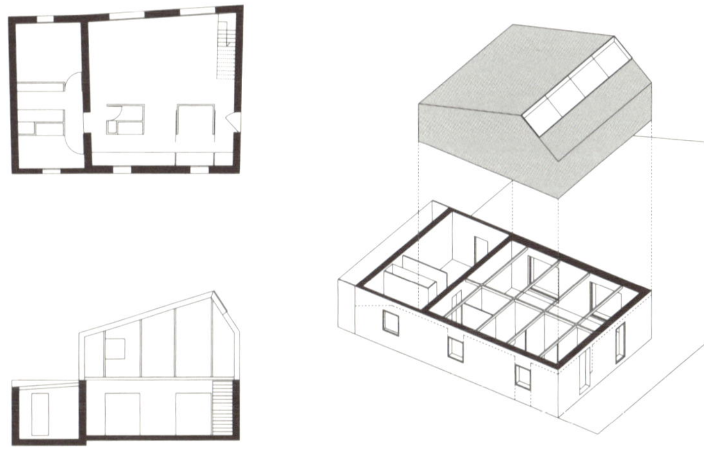

SEASIDE HOUSE

Concrete or wood? Take both and let them look similar.

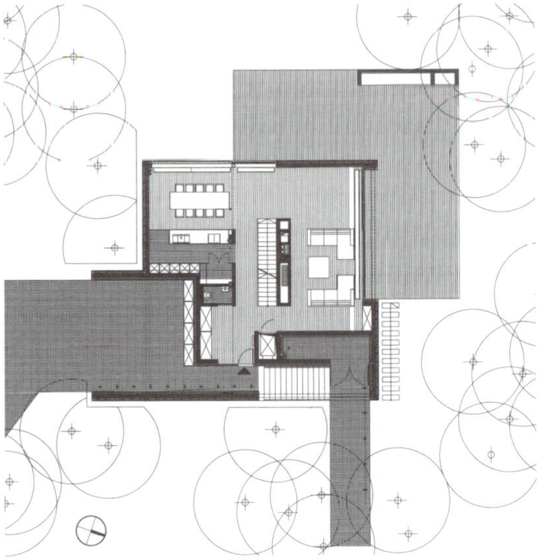

Architects | Ultra Architects / Marcin Kościuch, Tomasz Osięgłowski
Location | Baltic Sea Coast, Poland
Completion | 2013
Size | 485 sqm

The cubic, monolithic shell of the house exudes a sense of safety, geometric stability and compactness. The building is located in a coastal town on a plot of land just behind a bank of sand dunes. Replacing the former residence, the new volume is carefully inserted between the site's pine trees (none of which were felled). Since the structure needed to be heavy and waterproof due to the instability of the ground and high ground water level the architects chose reinforced concrete as a main structural material. Rough, gray concrete acts as a natural finishing of interiors as well. The third construction material is sheet metal. The window frames and other components were designed in a graphite color.

The main idea was sincerity of material – the architects wanted to be true to the way concrete is used and looks. In addition to its structural aspect, concrete is also used for finishing the interiors. Its gray color and grainy texture with imprints of wooden formwork are balanced with white walls and wooden floors. In contrast to the interior, building façades are covered with wooden cladding. A characteristic reversal was achieved: warm wood on the outside and rough concrete on the inside.

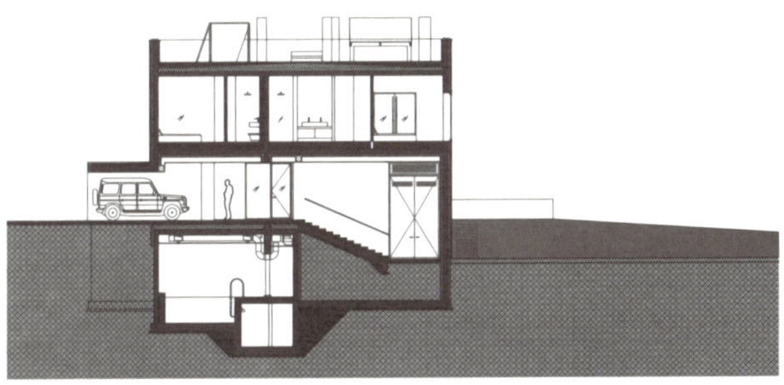

KHM26

Make a virtue of necessity. If only the result were always as impressive as this Frisian jewel.

Architects | Tim Piët Architect & Jos Blom
Location | Grou, The Netherlands
Completion | 2013
Size | 180 sqm

On the shore of the Frisian lake Pikmeer near Grouw Dutch architects Tim Piët and Jos Blom (formerly know as FLATarchitects) designed KHM26, a holiday home for a private client. With its vast meadows on one side and the openness of the lake on the other, the house is surrounded with a panoramic view. The compact and clear design enhances this grand view. The house is characterized by large glass façades and a tough cover of Corten steel. A concrete core organizes the floor-plan on the inside and emphasizes the entrance on the outside. With its natural and raw appearance the KHM26 fits well in the rugged beauty of its environment. KHM26 was nominated for the 2014 Dutch Steel Award.

MAMMOET

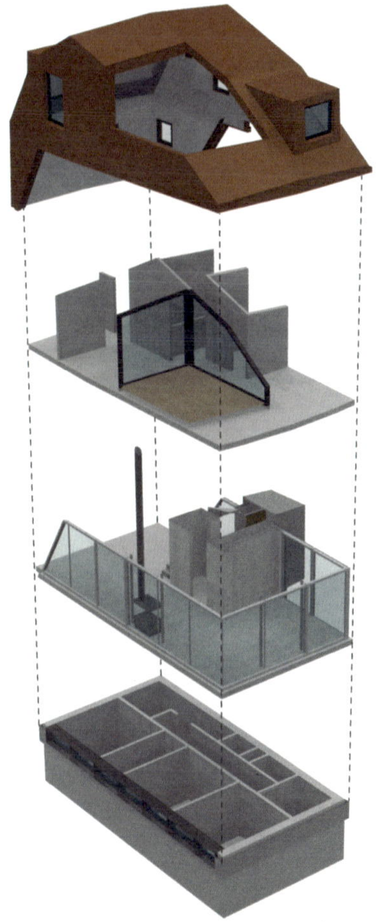

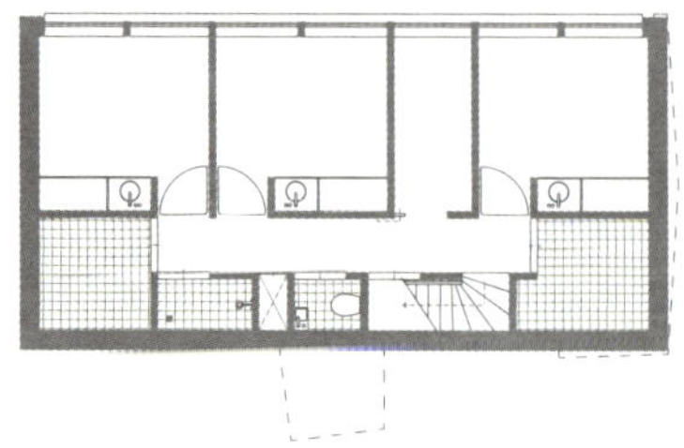
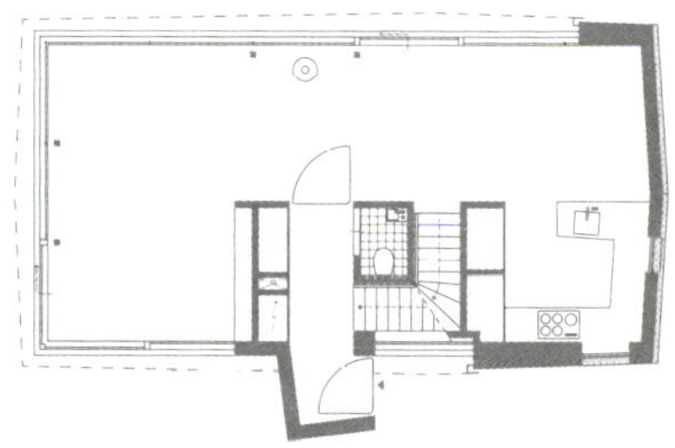
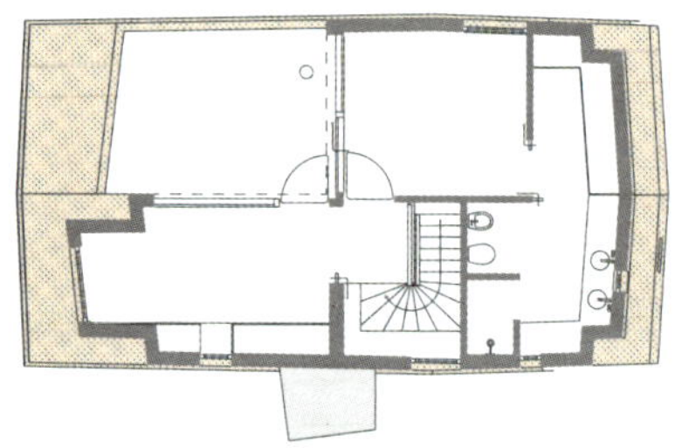

One of the consequences of the unique location at the edge of the lake was that the building site was hard to reach for construction. Therefore it was decided to build the house elsewhere. It then became possible to ensure high quality construction. There were also beneficial effects on the construction costs as well as protection of the sensitive location. The transportation of the 240 ton house was a spectacular affair.

CASTLE MUSEUM AND RESTAURANT AT THE LAKE

The perfection of a Swiss idyll. There is no better way to experience culture than dining in a historical setting.

Architects | Häberli-Architekten AG, Bern, Switzerland
Writer | Christoph Schläppi, Historian, Bern, Switzerland
Location | Restaurant Schloss Oberhofen, Oberhofen am Thunersee, Switzerland
Completion | 1855 / 1920 / 2014
Size | 240 sqm (restaurant)
Original use | service apartment, gatehouse, horse stables, remise

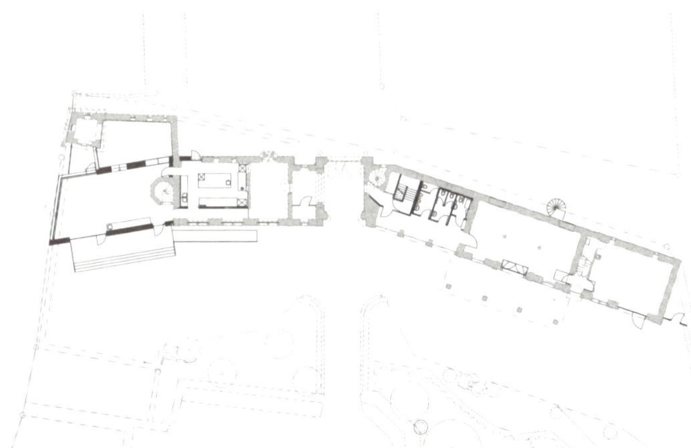

The building is a replacement on the lakeside in the ensemble of annexes of the medieval castle and lifestyle museum. Although it is a "by product" of the extensive building restoration, it contributes substantially to the attraction of the facility. Historic preservation, natural hazards, handicap access, and building regulations all created hurdles for construction. These had to be handled with much attention to detail and a time-consuming optimization process involving a synthesis of geometry, construction and technology. Because its expression of directness has positioned the building in the center of public awareness, the building has become a favorite of the operators and the visitors. With its cheerful and comfortable atmosphere and easy going presence the building was accepted from the start.

The simple contours and openings of the concrete cube with raw formwork enrich the tourist spot with an excursion restaurant which serves exclusive cuisine in the evening. With its mineral materiality, scale and subtle floor plan geometry the building respectfully assumes a place of distinction in the historic ensemble. In doing so it creates an ideal stage for the experience of the picturesque castle and unique landscape.

DOMunder

Travel back in time accompanied by state-of-the-art materials and techniques.

DOMunder wants to exhibit the grandeur of twenty centuries of history, and to allow visitors to perceive the impact of the collapsed portion of the Dom Church: the size of the nave, the extent of the foundations and the building techniques from centuries ago. The goal is to literally take the visitors back in time, by taking them from the ground level of the square to the distant past. Nowhere else in the Netherlands can twenty centuries of history be experienced at a single venue. While using an interactive torch the visitors descend into the darkness in search of the remnants that re-tell the stories of Domplein. DOMunder enables visitors to take a trip back in time.

Architects | JDdVarchitects
Location | Domplein, Utrecht, The Netherlands
Completion | 2014
Size | 350 sqm

DOM
UNDER

UNDER

The monocoque lining is perforated with a numerically controlled range of hundreds of thousands of different-sized little holes. By backlighting these, together they form pointillist images of historical scenes in combination with projections.

VILLA SK

A house or a loft? Why choose when you can have both!

Architects | Atelier Thomas Pucher
Location | Graz, Austria
Completion | 2011
Size | 240 sqm

Three materials are used for the addition – large plates of glass, rough stones and reddish concrete. The concrete structure of the roof is framed by two steel trusses which extend almost to the boundary of the property. Although the roof structure is supported by narrow metal pieces, it seems to float over the stone wall, creating a delicate contrast between the various elements and materials. This gentle gesture includes a walnut tree on the property and creates an area of quiet and privacy. The large green areas generate an intimate connection between the interior and an outside area which has been changing for decades. The resulting interweaving of nature and architecture provides a comfortable and harmonic background for family life.

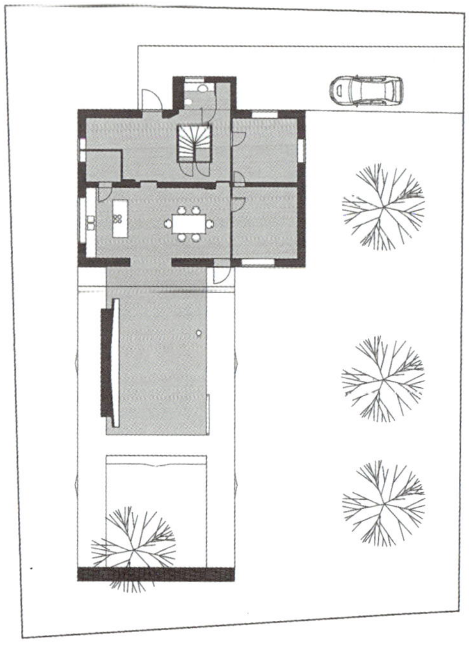

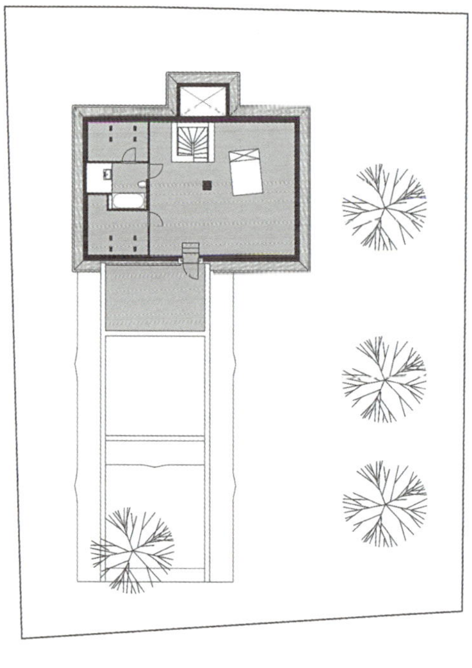

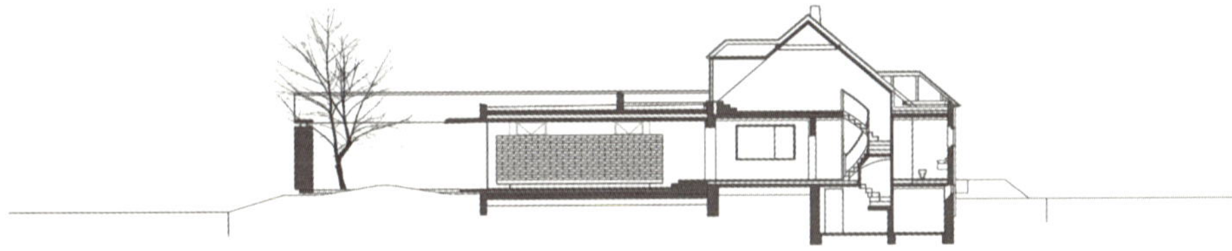

The original task for the Villa SK was to rebuild an existing one family house in order to meet the future demands of the residents within a strict budget. Instead of radically reorganizing the old structure of the house, the decision was made to build an addition contrasting with the existing building which would extend the living room into the garden.

ARZERGRANDE RENOVATION / CASONE AZZURRO AND NEW PAVILION

Go green! Here is proof that eco-friendly and stylish go together quite naturally.

Architects | 3NDY STUDIO
Location | Via San Marco 3, Arzergrande (Padua), Italy
Completion | 2014
Size | 90 sqm
Original use | farmhouse

At the end of 2014 3ndy studio completed the conservative restructuring of the rural thatched house "Casone Azzurro" and the new pavilion to accommodate tourists. The whole complex offers a unique experience for the general public. The "Casone Azzurro" is an outstanding example of a green building that recalls the unique rural housing typology of the pre-industrial age in the Padua Province. 3ndy Studio oversaw the recently completed restoration of the entire Casone and has implemented the project for the new tourist pavilion, located in the same area. The new pavilion is inspired by the surrounding environment and adopts the shapes and colors that already exist in nature, interpreting the rural world of which the Casone has been a part.

The Casone is made of materials found in nature: walls are made of a mix of sun-dried clays, dung, straw and lime, whereas the thatched roof is made of rye straw and reeds, requiring maintenance every 20 years. The grove of reeds, like a sketch of repeated vertical elements forming a dense brown-green wall, inspired the creation of the main façade of the pavilion and the key element of the building.

In the immediate vicinity the almost shockingly modern annex with the red exposed concrete and a flat roof disrupts the staid life under the gables. The small estate house from the 1950s, which is the basis for this apartment house extension, is not 'knocked off' with 21st century technology. Instead, its development is independent and contemporary. For instance the interior features are completely new: the suddenness of large openings, greater views, multi-story penetrations in contrast to the smaller scale and narrowness of the past. The ensemble's charm, including a new carport, consists in contrast and interaction. Different construction data logically lead to architecturally different results.

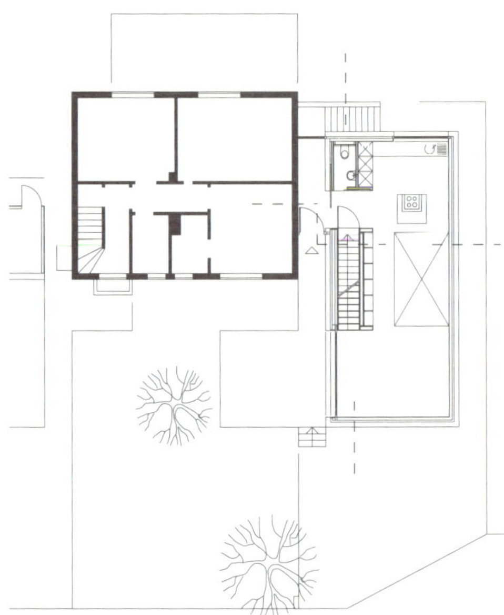

PUEBLO HOUSE

This reinterpretation of a duplex house offers a great deal of flexibility for three generations.

Architect | Matti Schmalohr DI Architekt BDA DWB
Location | Oelde, Germany
Completion | 2006
Size | 95 sqm

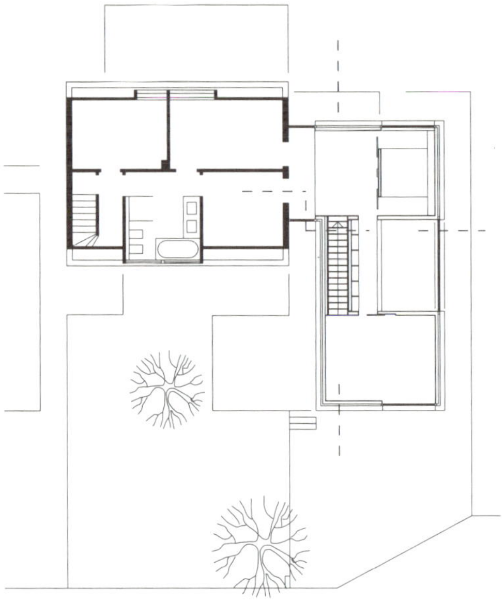

Iron oxide red exposed concrete, even as a fifth façade. This pueblo house consists of exposed concrete, glass and window frames. Everything left out saves material and does not need maintenance or painting. Inside there are no accessories, with the smooth wall and furniture surfaces meeting in a shadow gap.

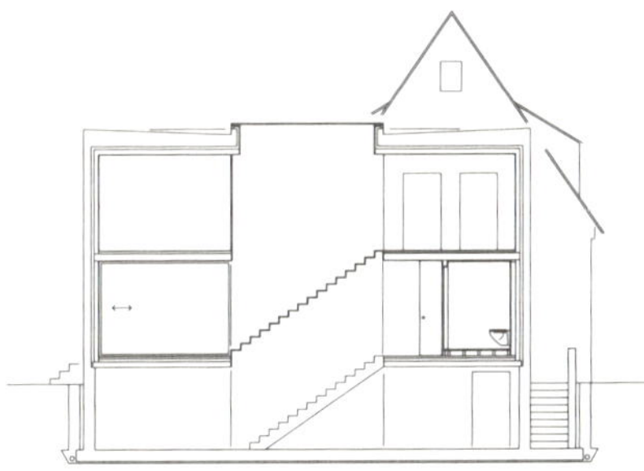

FASHION HOUSE GARHAMMER

Town wall meets brass and steel meets rust look. A fashion paradise between tradition and modern world.

Architects | Blocher Blocher Partners
Location | Marktplatz 28, 94065 Waldkirchen, Germany
Completion | 1896 / 2013
Size | 9,000 sqm
Original use | grocery store

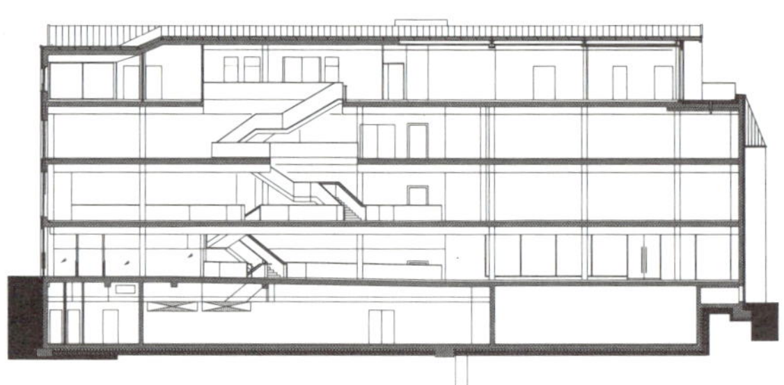

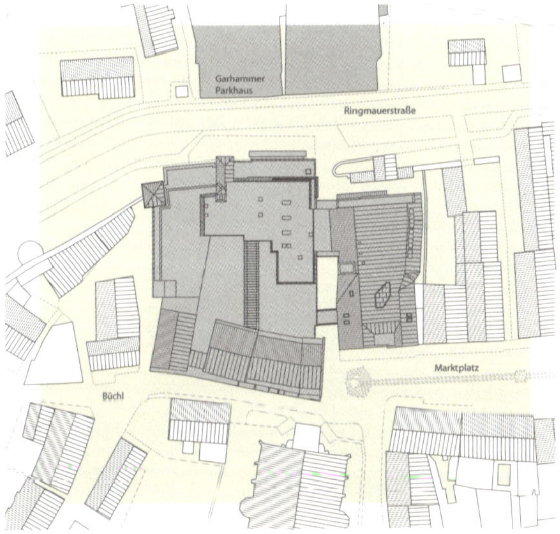

It has been expanded from 2500 to 9000 square meters, modernized, compacted and crowned with a gourmet restaurant. In its multi-faceted style Garhammer in Waldkirchen in Lower Bavaria combines village history with metropolitan flair. The numerous entrances, exits and passageways open up the fashion center to the village around it or bring it in. The creative interaction with historical buildings, contemporary materials and decorative elements leads to diverse worlds of shopping and experience, all staged in the intriguing context of varying room heights, airspaces and shopping levels. The result is a contemporary commercial property where selection and stylistic certainty are on a par with consulting and service.

The spatial arrangement follows the natural characteristics of the property's sloping topography. Through the split-level construction, a juxtaposition of different levels emerges, each highly individualized and offering exciting vantages of its neighbors. The design of Modehaus Garhammer is a fitting counterpart to the historically protected village ensemble, with its squares, alleys and stairways.

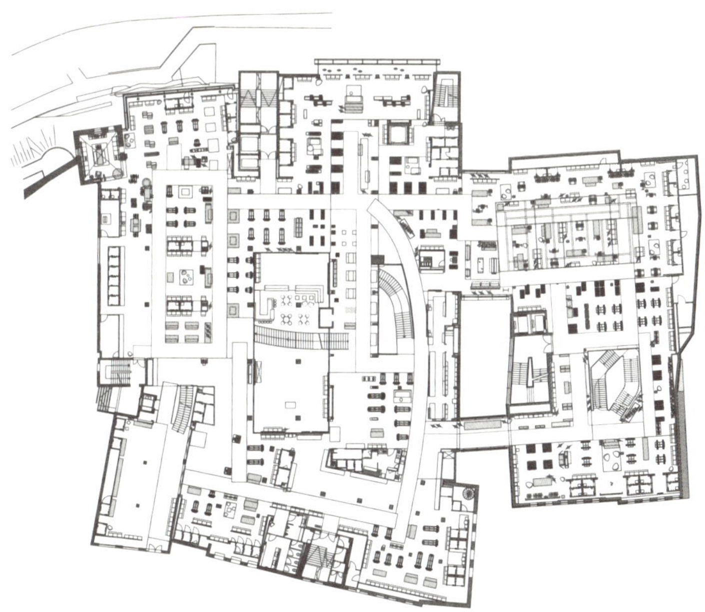

HOUSE IN ISHIKIRI

For the real open air feeling ... all year round!

Rough concrete walls and a black archetypal house above it, a translucent lean-to roof, a white high flat roof and a silver box underneath it: these totally different materials, colors and volumes are combined to form the House in Ishikiri. The site is in a residential area developed around 1930, which overlooks the urban area of Osaka Plain. The architects were attracted to the fine mosaic pattern of old and rebuilt houses that told a history of over eighty years. Firstly, the concrete walls with rough texture were built by using horizontally stacked luan plywood strips as formwork to match the old masonry and concrete-block walls in the area. Then, following the roof shape of houses in the neighborhood, a black archetypal house was mounted on top of them. The space for a kitchen and a bathroom is created between the concrete walls and the cliff-retaining wall behind the house, finished with a translucent lean-to roof and wooden windows and doors.

Architects | Tato Architects / Yo Shimada
Location | Osaka, Japan
Completion | 2013
Size | 99 sqm

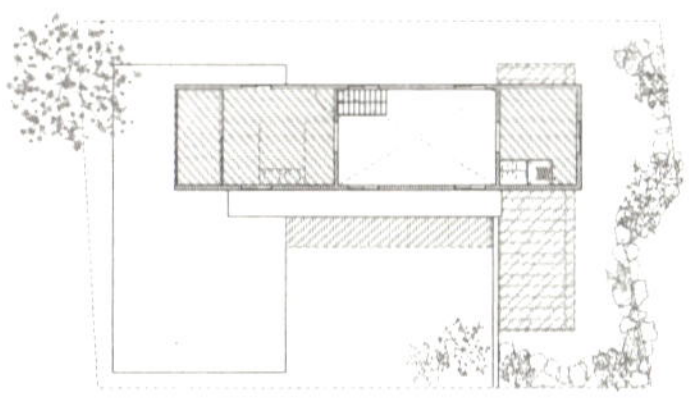

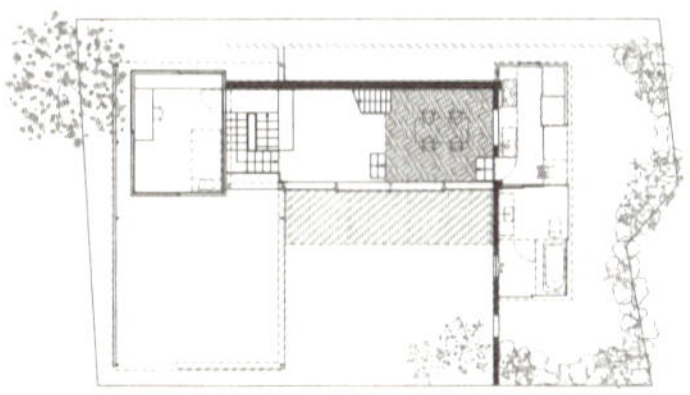

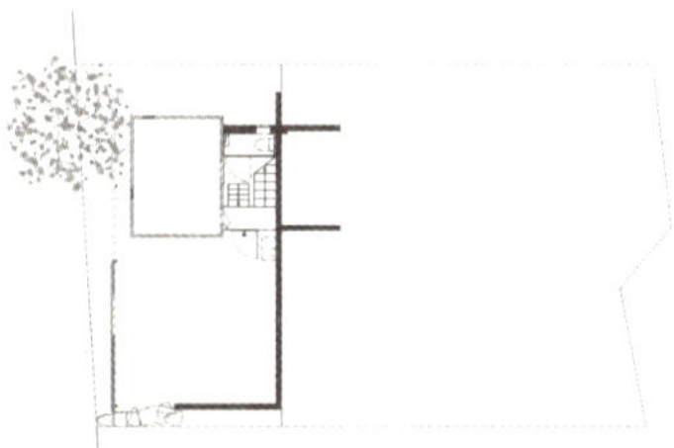

As the client requested an open-air feeling to their bathroom, the architects designed the faintly luminous roof on the bathroom and kitchen by inserting translucent insulation, which has better thermal insulation characteristics, between glass and multi-layered polycarbonate, than glass fiber wool.

INDEX

INDEX

PICTURE CREDITS

Maira Acayaba 224–227
Fernando Alda, Seville 9 l., 14–17, 403 b., 405 l.
Pau Ardèvol, Barcelona 322, 324 a., 325 a.
BAST 410–413
Peter Bennetts 23–25
Luc Boegly, Paris 102–105
Andreas Bormann 306–309
Esteve Bosch, Girona 323
Yvonne Brandwijk 290–293
Jeremi Buczkowski / Ultra Architects 414–417
Barabara Bühler, Vaduz 270, 271 l., 273 r.
Tamás Bujnovszky 9 r., 66–71
BUREAU A 47
José L. Caballano 402
Javier Callejas 228–231
Alejandro Cartagena 152–155
Chaoz 266–269
Tibor Dékány 9 r., 66–71
Henrik Diemann 82–85
Digidaan, Amsterdam 144–147
Filip Dujardin 58–61
George Dupin 338–341
Alexander Dzurec, Santa Fe 204
Damir Fabijanić 378–381
FAF studio 254–257
Ashley Feldman, Melbourne 374–377
Andrés Flajszer 310–313
Johan Fowelin, Stockholm 10–13
Martí Franch, Girona 324 b., 325 b.
Roger Frei 212–215
Nathan Gallagher 259 b., 261 b.
Sergio Garcia 9 r., 66–71
Xose Garrido 403 a., 404, 405 b. r.
Alexander Gempeler, Bern 422–425
Régis Golay, FEDERAL Studio, Geneva 128–131
John Gollings 22
Adrià Goula, Barcelona 118–121, 172–175
Adrian Gramunt, Lausanne 271 b. r., 272 a., 273 b. l.
Jesus Granada 176–179
Tim Greatrex 258, 259 a., 260, 261 a.
Stéphane Groleau 72–75
Fernando Guerra, Lisbon – Ultimas Reportagens 8, 76–81, 160–163, 242–245, 298, 301
Adam Hatvani 9 r., 66–71
Ester Havlová, Prag 216–219
Bertil Hertzberg 274–277
José Hévia 86–89
Fabian Hild, Frankfurt am Main 442–445
Anders Hviid, Denmark 318–321
Relja Ivanic, Mokrin 110–113
Wolfgang Janzer 370–373
K&L Architekten, St. Gallen 272 b. l., b. r.
Pedro Kok, São Paulo 48–51
Kurt Kuball 302–305
Jan Kuděj 262–265
Marion Lafogler, Bozen 184–187
Martin Lässig, Köln 294–297
Liky Foto 90–93, 354–357
Åke E:son Lindman, Lindman Photography 36–39
Arend Loerts, Leeuwarden 418, 419 b. r., 420 a. l., 421
Francisco López 405 a. r.
Justin Maconochie www.jmaconochie.com 398–401
John J. Macualay, Milwaukee, Wisconsin 232–235
Marcello Mariana 136–139
Benedikt Markel, Prague 124–127, 156–159
Janez Marolt, Ljubljana 140–143
Thomas Mayer, Neuss 164–167, 358–361
Simon Menges, Berlin 18–21
Wai Ming Ng 106–109
Stefan Müller, Berlin 114–117
Jeroen Musch bzw. Krill-Christian Müller Architects 406–409
Sun Namgoong 382–385
Yatri Niehaus, Berlin 32–35
Tatsuya Noaki 394–397
Klemens Ortmeyer 390–393
Pedro Pegenaute 299–300
Dylan Perrenoud 44–46
Tim Piët Architect & Jos Blom 419 a. l., 420 b. l.
point 4 space/cosmin dragomir 282–285
Eugeni Pons 346–349, 386–389
Nani Pujol photographer 168–171
Alfonso Quiroga 236–241
Reiulf Ramstad Arkitekter 52–55
Kate Russell, Santa Fe 205 a., 206–207
SABO project, New York 188–191
Lukas Schaller 430–433
Albrecht Imanuel Schnabel, Rankweil 132–135
Oliver Schuh / Palladium Photodesign 426–429
Richard John Seymour 148–151, 200–203
Su Shengliang 180–183
Daisuke Shimokawa / Nacása&Partners Inc 330–333
Shinkenchikusha, Tokyo 446–449
Gustavo Sosa Pinilla 196–199
Riccardo Spinello photographer, Padua 434–437
Stamers Kontor 94–97
StijnStijl 40–43
Jordi Surroca 28–31
Bujnovszky Tamás 192–195
THE BLACK RABBIT, Mexico 220–223
Dominique Uldry 208–211, 342–345
Conné van d'Grachten, Ulm 250–253
Walter Vielain 326–329
Ruedi Walti, Basel 350–353
Harry Weber 278–281
Mario Webhofer, Aldrans 314–317
Dominique Wehrli 334–337
Klaus Dieter Weiss, Minden 438–441
Volker Wortmeyer, Nordholz 286–289
Toshiyuki Yano 246–249, 366–369
Montse Zamorano architecture photography 62–65
Stefan Zenzmaier, Kuchl 98–101

All other pictures were made available by the architects and designers.

Cover front: Fernando Guerra, Lisbon – Ultimas Reportagens
Cover back: Justin Maconochie

IMPRINT

The Deutsche Nationalbibliothek lists this publication in the Deutsche Nationalbibliografie; detailed bibliographic data are available in the Internet at http://dnb.dnb.de

ISBN 978-3-03768-195-4

www.braun-publishing.ch

1st edition 2015

Editor: Sibylle Kramer
Editorial staff and layout: Helen Gührer, Alessia Calabrò
Translation: Geoffrey Steinherz
Graphic concept: Michaela Prinz, Berlin
Reproduction: Bild1Druck GmbH, Berlin